NATIONAL 4 & 5

HISTORY

THE ATLANTIC SLAVE TRADE 1770–1807

SECOND EDITION

Jerry Teale

Series Editor: John A. Kerr

DYNAMIC LEARNING

HODDER GIBSON
AN HACHETTE UK COMPANY

The Publishers would like to thank the following for permission to reproduce copyright material:

Photo credits
p.2 © Eddie Mulholland/REX/Shutterstock; **p.4** © Print Collector/Hulton Archive/Getty Images; **p.6** © Granger, NYC/TopFoto; **p.11** (left) © APIC/Getty Images, (right) © SSPL/Getty Images; **p.12** © Werner Forman/Universal Images Group/Getty Images; **p.13** (left) © De Agostini/Getty Images, (right) De Agostini/Getty Images; **p.14** Granger, NYC/TopFoto; **p.15** (top) © Corbis Historical/Getty Images, (bottom) © Fotosearch/Getty Images; **p.16** © Jackson, William (1730-1803)/Walker Art Gallery, National Museums Liverpool/Bridgeman Images; **pp.16–18** (inset) © Robert Kneschke/Fotolia; **pp.17–18** (inset) © Ljupco Smokovski/Fotolia; **p.17** (bottom) © Images of Africa Photobank/Alamy Stock Photo; **p.18** (top) © LIONEL HEALING/Stringer/AFP/Getty Images, (bottom) © Library of Congress Prints and Photographs Division; **p.21** (top) © Historical Picture Archive/CORBIS/Corbis via Getty Images, (bottom) © BLM Collection/Alamy Stock Photo; **p.26** © Spencer Arnold/Getty Images; **p.27** © Mary Evans Picture Library; **p.28** (top) © Richard Naude/Alamy Stock Photo, (bottom) © Hulton Archive/Getty Images; **p.29** (top) © Universal History Archive/Getty Images, (bottom) © Sabena Jane Blackbird/Alamy Stock Photo; **p.32** (left) © Geraint Lewis/Alamy Stock Photo, (right) © CSG CIC Glasgow Museums Collection; **p.33** © By permission of University of Glasgow Library, Special Collections; **p.34** © CSG CIC Glasgow Museums Collection; **p.35** (top left) © Matthew Oldfield Travel Photography/Alamy Stock Photo, (bottom left) © British Library Board. All Rights Reserved/Bridgeman Images, (right) ian woolcock/Alamy Stock Photo; **p.42** (top) © Hulton Archive/Getty Images, (bottom) © Time Life Pictures/Timepix/The LIFE Images Collection/Getty Images; **p.45** © Pat Canova/Alamy Stock Photo; **p.46** (top) © Granger, NYC/TopFoto, (bottom) © Rischgitz/Getty Images; **p.47** © Chronicle/Alamy Stock Photo; **p.49** © CORBIS/Corbis via Getty Images; **p.50** (top) © British Library Board. All Rights Reserved/Bridgeman Images, (bottom left) © Fotosearch/Getty Images, (bottom right) © MPI/Getty Images; **p.51** TopFoto/HIP; **p.55** © DEA PICTURE LIBRARY/Getty Images; **p.57** © (left) © Granger, NYC/TopFoto, (right) © Granger, NYC/TopFoto; **p.62** © Beinecke Rare Book and Manuscript Library, Yale University; **p.63** © Granger, NYC/TopFoto; **p.64** © Universal History Archive/Getty Images; **p.70** © Hulton Archive/Getty Images; **p.71** © British Library Board. All Rights Reserved/Bridgeman Images; **p.76** (top) © Fotosearch/Getty Images, (right) AF archive/Alamy Stock Photo; **p.77** (left) © Granger, NYC/TopFoto, (top right) © DEA PICTURE LIBRARY/Getty Images, (bottom right) Lordprice Collection/Alamy Stock Photo; **p.78** © Historical Picture Archive/CORBIS/Corbis via Getty Images; **p.79** © Hulton Archive/Getty Images; **p.80** Internet Archive (archive.org); **p.81** © Wilberforce House, Hull City Museums and Art Galleries, UK/The Bridgeman Art Library; **p.83** © Lordprice Collection/Alamy Stock Photo; **p.87** © Michael Graham-Stewart/Bridgeman Images; **p.88** © Private Collection/Bridgeman Images; **p.89** © Private Collection/Courtesy of Swann Auction Galleries/Bridgeman Images; **p.92** © AF archive/Alamy Stock Photo; **p.93** (top) © Royal Albert Memorial Museum, Exeter, Devon, UK/Bridgeman Images, (bottom) © Illustrated London News Ltd/Mary Evans; **p.94** © Prisma UIG/Getty Images; **p.98** (top) © Benjamin Lowy/Getty Images Reportage, (bottom) © Sovfoto/Universal Images Group/REX/Shutterstock; **p.99** © Anton Vasilkovsky/Fotolia; **p.100** (left and right) Everett Collection Inc./Alamy Stock Photo.

Acknowledgements: See page 106 for text acknowledgements.
Every effort has been made to trace all copyright holders, but if any have been inadvertently overlooked the Publishers will be pleased to make the necessary arrangements at the first opportunity.

Although every effort has been made to ensure that website addresses are correct at time of going to press, Hodder Gibson cannot be held responsible for the content of any website mentioned in this book. It is sometimes possible to find a relocated web page by typing in the address of the home page for a website in the URL window of your browser.

Hachette UK's policy is to use papers that are natural, renewable and recyclable products and made from wood grown in sustainable forests. The logging and manufacturing processes are expected to conform to the environmental regulations of the country of origin.

Orders: please contact Bookpoint Ltd, 130 Park Drive, Milton Park, Abingdon, Oxon OX14 4SE.
Telephone: (44) 01235 827827. Fax: (44) 01235 400454. Lines are open 9.00–5.00, Monday to Saturday, with a 24-hour message answering service. Visit our website at www.hoddereducation.co.uk.
Hodder Gibson can be contacted directly at hoddergibson@hodder.co.uk

Cover photo: © Morozova Tatiana/123RF.com
Illustrations by Gray Publishing
Produced and typeset in 11/11.5pt Folio Light by Integra Software Services Pvt. Ltd., Pondicherry, India
Printed in Slovenia

A catalogue record for this title is available from the British Library

ISBN: 978 1 5104 2931 4

FSC
www.fsc.org
MIX
Paper from responsible sources
FSC™ C104740

Contents

Preface

This is one of a series of six titles fully updated for the National 4 & 5 History courses to be assessed from 2018 onwards. Students should study three main sections in National 4 & 5 History, with a very wide selection of topics to choose from (five in the first two, ten in the third). The series covers two topics in each section.

The six titles in the series are:

▶ National 4 & 5 History: Migration and Empire 1830–1939
▶ National 4 & 5 History: The Era of the Great War 1900–1928
▶ National 4 & 5 History: The Atlantic Slave Trade 1770–1807
▶ National 4 & 5 History: Changing Britain 1760–1914
▶ National 4 & 5 History: Hitler and Nazi Germany 1919–1939
▶ National 4 & 5 History: Free at Last? Civil Rights in the USA 1918–1968

Each book contains comprehensive coverage of the four SQA key issue areas for National 5, as well as guidance and practice on Assignment writing and assessment procedures.

The Assignment: what you need to know

National 5

What is the Assignment for National 5?

The Assignment is written under exam conditions and then sent to the SQA to be marked. It counts for 20 marks out of a total of 100, so doing well in the Assignment can provide you with a very useful launchpad for overall success in the National 5 exam.

The Assignment has two stages:

▶ research (the gathering together of your findings and sources) – this can be done at any appropriate point during your course
▶ production of evidence (the writing up, in exam conditions, in the allotted one-hour sitting).

How should I write my Assignment?

You are given marks for showing certain skills in your Assignment. First, you must choose a question to write about. That means it should end with a question mark, using phrases such as 'How fully … ', 'How successful … ' or 'To what extent was … '. This will steer you into researching a topic and reaching a conclusion rather than simply writing a description of something.

Once your question is sorted, you must aim to:

▶ Write an introduction that sets the context for your question and which outlines different, relevant factors.
▶ Organise your information so that it makes sense as a balanced answer to your main question.

- Use your own knowledge and understanding to explain and analyse the question you have chosen.
- Use information gathered from *at least* two relevant sources to address and support these factors. For example, two books or one book and an interview.
- Use other detailed information to support these.
- Evaluate which of the factors were more important than others.
- Identify and assess different perspectives and/or points of view (try to include *at least* two).
- Reach a conclusion that states what you think is the main answer to your question.
- Give reasons to support your conclusion.

What should I write about?

Here are some suggestions for suitable questions based on the content of this book:

- ✓ How important was the role of African leaders in organising the Atlantic slave trade?
- ✓ To what extent can Liverpool's success in the Atlantic slave trade be explained by its geographical position?
- ✓ To what extent does the labour shortage in the Caribbean explain the growth of the Atlantic slave trade?
- ✓ How important was poor diet as a reason for loss of life among slaves on the middle passage?
- ✓ How successful was London compared to other ports involved in the Atlantic slave trade?
- ✓ To what extent was running away the main form of resistance on the plantations?
- ✓ How important was the case of the *Zong* to the growth of the abolitionist movement?
- ✓ To what extent was William Wilberforce responsible for the success of the abolitionist campaign?
- ✓ To what extent was the fear of slave rebellion responsible for the ending of the slave trade in 1807?

The following list contains examples of badly worded Assignment questions:

- ✗ What was the triangular trade?
- ✗ What were the effects of the slave trade on Africa?
- ✗ Why was Bristol heavily involved in the slave trade in 1770 but less involved by 1807?
- ✗ How was sugar produced during the time of the slave trade?
- ✗ In what ways did slaves resist their captors on the middle passage?
- ✗ Why was the middle passage a terrible experience for slaves?
- ✗ What part did William Wilberforce play in the abolitionist movement?
- ✗ What methods were used by abolitionists in their campaign against the slave trade?
- ✗ What arguments were used by opponents of the abolitionist movement?

These are just headings. They are bad either because they are too broad in scope or because they focus on areas that will not offer you the opportunity to gain maximum marks.

Be safe! There are no prizes for giving yourself a difficult question that you have made up yourself. Choose something from the history you have already been studying. You could choose a title from a past exam paper: www.sqa.org.uk/sqa/47447 or modify a past paper question, with help from your teacher. Avoid doing something risky – you only get one chance at this Assignment.

How long should my Assignment be?

Your Assignment has no word count limit – it all depends on how much you can write in the permitted hour. Most Assignments are about four or five pages long.

Remember that you also have a Resource Sheet to help you

On your Resource Sheet you will list the sources that you will refer to in your Assignment. This will show the marker that you have researched, selected and organised your information.

Your Resource Sheet will be sent to the SQA with your finished Assignment. You will not be given a mark for your completed Resource Sheet, but markers will use it to see that you have done the necessary research and have found appropriate sources to use in your Assignment. The Resource Sheet is *yours*. You can change it, colour it or print it out. You can write it anywhere, anytime before you write your Assignment under exam conditions. You can include bullet points, spidergrams (spider diagrams), notes, names and dates. The only strict rules are that your Resource Sheet must:

- not be longer than 200 words
- be on one side of A4 paper
- contain the title and author of *at least* two sources you are referring to in your Assignment.

You must **not** copy large sections from your Resource Sheet into your Assignment, but you **can** copy across quotes from sources you have on your Resource Sheet.

National 4: Added Value Unit

The Assignment (sometimes called the Added Value Unit) lets you show off your skills as you research a historical issue. You have a lot of choice in what you can investigate and you can also choose to present your findings in different ways. That means you don't *have* to write an essay to demonstrate your skills, knowledge and understanding.

To be successful in National 4 you have to show you can research and use information by doing the following things:

- Choosing an appropriate historical theme or event for study. Your teacher can help you choose.
- Collecting relevant evidence from *at least* two sources of information.
- Organising and using the information that you have collected to help you write about the subject you have chosen.
- Describing what your chosen subject is about.
- Explaining why your chosen subject happened (its cause) or explaining what happened next because of your chosen subject (its effects).

As you work through this book you will make mobiles, give presentations, and create posters, diagrams and artwork. All these things could be part of your National 4 Assignment. You then have to present your findings.

Don't worry – if you get stuck your teacher is allowed to give you help and advice at *any stage* as you do your Assignment.

Do I have to write a long essay?

No, you don't. You can choose how you present your Assignment at National 4. For example, you could give a talk and then be asked some questions about your subject by your teacher. You could do a PowerPoint presentation or keep a learning log. You might decide to design a poster or use some other way to display your work. But yes, you *could* write an essay if you wanted to!

1 Introduction

What is this course about?

The reason there is such a strong link between the **West Indies** and West Africa is the slave trade and the use of slaves in the Caribbean that existed until the nineteenth century.

In this book you will find out why slavery was used in the Caribbean and its effects on Britain and the Caribbean islands. You will discover how captured people from West Africa were treated on the **middle passage**, how they were sold into slavery and how they were treated on the **plantations** where they worked.

Finally, there is a close examination of the personalities and the methods used in the **abolitionists**' campaign to end the Atlantic slave trade.

> **GLOSSARY**
>
> **West Indies** islands of the Caribbean Sea
>
> **Middle passage** the journey from West Africa to the West Indies, the second part of the triangular trade route
>
> **Plantation** an estate where crops such as coffee, tobacco or sugar are grown
>
> **Abolitionists** people who wanted to end the slave trade

What will this book help me to do?

This book will help you to be successful in your National 4 and 5 History course. It contains everything you need to know about all key issues and descriptions of content outlined by the SQA for 'The Atlantic Slave Trade 1770–1807'.

The book provides advice and examples to help you answer all the different types of questions you are likely to face in the National 5 exam.

Finally, this book will provide guidance to help you work on the Assignment tasks.

The West Indies

Most people living in the West Indies can trace their ancestry back to West Africa. Even today the African influence is still strong. It can be detected in the languages that the people of the West Indies speak.

West African heritage can be seen in other ways. The champion athlete Usain Bolt comes from Trelawny parish in Jamaica. When he was interviewed by the *Daily Mail* newspaper about his record-breaking 100 m performance in 2009, he said that his success was partly due to his West African roots:

The guys back in the day were so strong from physical work … the genes are really strong.

US sprinter Michael Johnson, who is of West African descent, also believes that athletes like him have a unique genetic inheritance. Johnson argued that descendants of slaves from West Africa have a 'superior athletic gene'.

Why are there so many connections between the West Indies and West Africa?

This book will describe the movement of millions of people from West Africa to the islands of the West Indies. It will explain why these people were forced to work in a new land far from their homes. This is sometimes referred to as the 'African Holocaust', a description that compares the experience of Africans to that of the Jewish victims of Nazism. However, this is not an accurate description as the intention was to enslave rather than to commit mass murder. The term *Maafa*, a Kiswahili word meaning 'disaster', provides a more appropriate description. Kiswahili is a West African language sometimes called Swahili.

Use the internet to find out more about Jamaican athletes and the reasons for their successes.

Usain Bolt of Jamaica after winning the 100m sprint at the 2012 London Olympics

2 Why were people from West Africa taken to the West Indies?

What is this chapter about?

This chapter describes the importance of sugar to the development of the West Indies. It explains why there was a growing demand for sugar in Europe. It then shows the difficulties involved in producing sugar and how these problems were solved.

By the end of this chapter you should be able to:

▶ Explain the connection between the production of sugar and the reasons why people were taken from West Africa to the West Indies.
▶ Describe the way in which the triangular trade was organised.

Slaves

Many of the sources in this book use the word 'slaves' to describe the Africans affected by the Atlantic trade. It is important to remember that these people did not necessarily accept that they were slaves and fought against their enslavement in many ways. For that reason the term 'enslaved people' is used wherever possible.

So, why were people from West Africa taken to the West Indies? The short answer lies in a food you probably eat every day and something that happened for hundreds of years between the 1500s and the 1800s. That food is sugar. The thing that happened was the Atlantic slave trade, also known as the triangular trade.

Why was sugar so important in the story of West Indian slavery?

The world had known about sugar for a long time. By the sixth century AD, sugar cultivation and processing had reached the Middle East; then it was spread to countries around the Mediterranean by Arabs who traded sugar with Europe. Originally, people chewed raw **sugar cane** to extract its sweetness. The flavour was very attractive to people whose food was often tasteless, sour and rotten. The problem was that sugar was very difficult to produce in large amounts and it was also very expensive.

The big breakthrough in sugar production began when Christopher Columbus 'discovered' the **New World**: in other words, Europeans had reached America. The year was 1492.

> **GLOSSARY**
>
> **Sugar cane** a tropical plant with a thick stem from which sugar can be extracted
>
> **New World** the area of the Americas discovered by Europeans in the fifteenth century

> Who are the people on the left of the picture? What have they laid down on the ground at their feet? What are the man in the centre of the picture (probably Columbus) and the man kneeling on the right both doing? What is the artist telling us about Columbus' first meeting with the people of the 'New World'?

This print from 1820 shows Christopher Columbus arriving in the 'New World'

Columbus was really looking for a short route to India by going westwards from Europe across the Atlantic Ocean. When Columbus' ship, the *Santa Maria*, ran aground on a large island in the Caribbean, he thought he had reached India so the islands became known as the 'West Indies'.

The Queen of Spain had sponsored Columbus' voyage but only on the understanding that any lands he discovered would belong to Spain. As a result, Columbus named the island La Isla Española ('The Spanish Island'). It soon became known as Hispaniola. Nowadays, the island is divided between two countries: Haiti and the Dominican Republic.

A map showing the islands of the Caribbean and the European countries that claimed them during the slave-trading era

When **gold** was discovered elsewhere in the New World, the Spanish became less interested in Hispaniola. However, on his second trip to the island, Columbus brought with him some sugar cane plants. Sugar cane was difficult to grow in Europe. Columbus hoped that this valuable crop would grow well in the island's tropical climate.

By the beginning of the sixteenth century, sugar was being grown on all of Spain's island colonies. By the start of the eighteenth century, sugar had become the most important product of the West Indies. When other European countries fought Spain and took over its West Indian islands, they kept on growing sugar.

> **GLOSSARY**
>
> **Gold** a precious metal sought after by European explorers in Africa in the fifteenth and sixteenth centuries

The sugar business

Sugar cane

Sugar cane grew well in the islands of the West Indies. However, extracting the sugar from sugar cane involved lots of people to grow, harvest and process the cane. It took 50 tons of sugar cane to make a ton of sugar. The following sources give you some idea of the difficulties. In the book, *The Slave Trade*, Josephine Kamm commented that:

Before planting canes, the land had to be made ready by burning and clearing away the grass. Rows of holes were then dug in which the new canes were planted. The base of each cane had to be covered with earth and then covered again regularly as the cane grew. The growing canes also had to be weeded constantly.

James Walvin noted in his book, also called *The Slave Trade*:

… once the cane was cut it had to be turned into crude sugar. It was crushed, boiled and distilled in a rough and often dangerous process which was as hard a task as working in the cane fields.

A drawing from about 1800 showing a group of enslaved African people in Jamaica, working in a factory to produce sugar from sugar cane

Who was used to produce the sugar?

Sugar production is very labour-intensive. That means very many people are needed to make it.

At first, the Spanish used the **Arawak** natives to work for them, but these gentle people gradually died out. It is thought that they were not immune to measles, smallpox and various fevers brought from Europe by the colonisers. Native Arawaks of the Caribbean were hunter-gatherers who were not used to farming.

Another supply of labour came from **bond servants**. Thousands of young British men and women signed contracts agreeing to work on sugar plantations for four to seven years. These bond servants would get free transportation to the West Indies and after working their contracts they were free to make new lives for themselves. However, the work was hard and many died on the journey or before their years were up. The harsh conditions were to blame, as the following source shows:

Bond servants mainly worked as field hands under the control of an overseer. They had to work from sun up to sun down. Due to disease, 50 to 75 per cent of bond servants were estimated to have died before their term had expired. Diseases such as malaria, yellow fever, dysentery, dropsy and **leprosy** *took their toll.*

Convicted criminals were also sent to the colonies to work on the sugar plantations. In the seventeenth century, Scotland produced a regular supply of workers who were sent to the colonies as a punishment rather than going to jail. Below is an edited extract from the court records of Jedburgh in 1666:

Robert Armstrong and Anthony Pott being indicted and accused of theft and various other crimes … and being found culpable and guilty of these crimes … are to be sent to Barbados and there to be sold as slaves and never to return to any of His Majesty's Dominions under pain of death.

GLOSSARY

Arawak a native people of the West Indies

Bond servants people forced to work for a period of time

Leprosy a contagious disease affecting the nerves and skin

Why were West Africans used for work in the West Indies?

The answer is that there were just not enough workers to keep up with the demand for sugar. Cane sugar had long been a luxury **commodity** in Europe. It was restricted to the very rich, who used it to sweeten exotic drinks such as coffee, tea and chocolate. Only small amounts of sugar cane could be grown in Cyprus, Crete, North Africa and southern Spain.

By the sixteenth and seventeenth centuries, improved standards of living had led to growing populations and economic change in European towns and cities. This increased the demand for more and more sugar.

As Europeans explored the Atlantic, they discovered new places that were very good for sugar cultivation. Cane was planted in Madeira and the Cape Verde islands. These were islands claimed by Portugal.

The Portuguese already had trade connections with West Africa, so when new workers were needed to replace those who did not survive the heavy work, it seemed natural to look to the African coast for labour. Africans were captured and forced to work on the islands.

A map showing the islands claimed by Spain and Portugal, where sugar was grown using enslaved people from West Africa

> ### GLOSSARY
>
> **Commodity** a product that can be bought or sold

Activity 1

Summarise this chapter

The following summary reminds you of what this chapter has been about. Words that are important have been made into ANAGRAMS. Your task is to sort out the anagrams and then write the correct version of this summary into your workbook or work file.

In 1492 Christopher Columbus landed on the island of **ALOHASNIPI**. The islands he discovered in this part of the New World became known as the **STEW SIDNIE**. Although there was little gold to be found, **GRUSA NACE** grew well here. The problem was finding **ROLAUB** to produce the sugar. The **VINEAT** people soon died out or fled. **NODB VERSANST** and **SNICTVOC** from Britain could be used. But as the **MADDEN** for sugar increased, planters made use of enslaved people from **STEW CRAFIA**.

Activity 2

If this is the answer, what is the question?

Below you will find a list of words or phrases. You have to make up a question that can only be answered by the word or phrase on the list. For example, if the word 'sugar' was the answer, a question could be 'What was the expensive commodity imported into Britain from the West Indies?'

- ▶ … the New World
- ▶ … because you need to weed it all the time
- ▶ … about 50 tons
- ▶ … Arawaks
- ▶ … well, it's got nothing to do with having to look after 007
- ▶ … it was an alternative to being sent to jail
- ▶ … worked on the Canaries
- ▶ … it made chocolate taste better

Activity 3

Work with a group. Imagine you are an **entrepreneur** living in Britain in the eighteenth century. You have made business connections with some sugar planters on the island of Barbados.

Produce a business plan showing how you would make maximum **profit** from the sugar business. Your plan should include:

- ▶ Name of the company
- ▶ Base/location
- ▶ Aims of the company
- ▶ Product
- ▶ Customers: Who? Where? Why will they buy it?
- ▶ Transport requirements
- ▶ Insurance requirements
- ▶ Labour: who will grow and process the sugar cane?
- ▶ Other staff
- ▶ Financial summary: likely costs and likely income.

How was the Atlantic slave trade organised?

The Atlantic Ocean is huge. The distance between West Africa and the West Indies is also enormous. How was it possible to organise the Atlantic slave trade? The answer to this question lies in something called the triangular trade.

The Atlantic slave trade is often called the triangular trade because there were three sides to it. When the routes taken by the ships involved in the trade were drawn on a map, they looked like the three sides of a triangle.

The transportation of enslaved Africans to the West Indies was part of the triangular trade. Ships travelled from Britain to West Africa, then to the West Indies and then back to Europe. On the first part of the trip, from Britain to Africa, the ships carried

> **GLOSSARY**
>
> **Entrepreneur** someone who is prepared to take risks in business
>
> **Profit** money earned from making a deal where the amount received is more than the amount spent

trade goods such as cloth, metal pots and pans, and guns. On the second part – known as the middle passage – enslaved Africans were taken to the West Indies. On the third and final stage, the ships brought back valuable goods such as sugar to Britain.

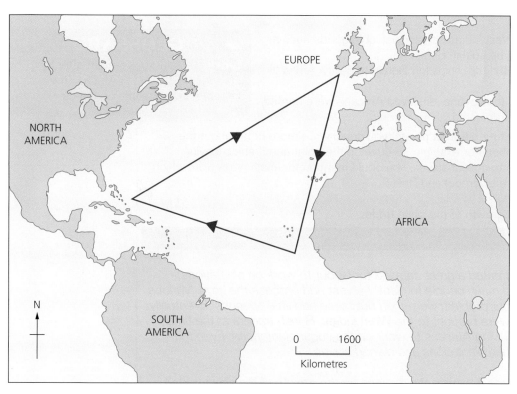

The triangular pattern of the Atlantic slave trade

Question practice

National 4

1 Describe the way in which sugar was produced in the West Indies during the eighteenth century.

Success criteria

Write an answer that gives at least two factual points of information about the way that sugar was produced in the West Indies during the eighteenth century.

2 Why were enslaved Africans taken to the West Indies in the 1770s?

Success criteria

Write an answer that provides at least two reasons to explain why enslaved Africans were taken to the West Indies.

National 5

1 Describe how the triangular trade was organised. (4 marks)

For a 'describe' question like this, success depends on you writing down four separate, accurate points of information that are relevant to the question asked.

Put these sentences in a more sensible order to produce a 4-mark answer.

- On this leg of the triangle, the ships carried trade goods such as cloth, metal pots and pans, and guns.
- The ships left the West Indies carrying valuable goods such as sugar and **ivory** to be sold in Britain.
- On the first part of the trip, ships left Britain to sail to Africa to collect slaves.
- On the next part of the voyage, enslaved Africans were carried to the West Indies to be sold.

> **GLOSSARY**
>
> **Ivory** elephant tusk sought after by European explorers in Africa in the fifteenth and sixteenth centuries

If you can't remember four different points, you could write more detail about the points you can remember. For example, to develop the point about ships leaving Britain to sail to Africa to collect slaves, you could mention the main ports from which they sailed, which were Liverpool and Bristol.

Source A is about the growth of the slave trade.

SOURCE A

The trade in sugar created a great demand for labour to work on plantations. Sugar cane required many people to plant, harvest and process the crop. Various solutions to the labour problem were tried but these had little success. Eventually, people from Africa were brought to the West Indies. British traders at the time saw no harm in enslaving Africans to work on the sugar plantations. Even the Church of England had plantations and owned slaves.

2 How fully does Source A explain the reasons for the growth of the slave trade? (6 marks)

This is a 'how fully' question. To be successful you need to make a clearly written judgement about how fully the source explains the growth of the slave trade. You can do that by writing: '*The source partly explains the reasons for the growth of the slave trade, but there were other reasons not mentioned in the source.*' This shows clearly that you are making a judgement.

You need to find at least three pieces of relevant information from the source which explain the growth of the slave trade. You could start with the point about the great demand for labour to work on the sugar plantations. Try to find two other points from the source.

To balance your answer, you then need to write at least three extra pieces of information from your own knowledge that are relevant to the question, but which have not been mentioned in the source. You could mention that there were not enough native people left in the Caribbean to grow the sugar cane that was needed. Try to come up with at least two more points to complete your answer.

3 What were the effects of the slave trade on Africa?

What is this chapter about?

This chapter describes slave trading in Africa from ancient times up until the 1700s. It considers what Europeans knew or believed about life in Africa and some of the myths that went around about West Africa. You will find out how much Africans themselves were involved in the Atlantic slave trade and what the effects of this trade were on Africa in the short term and the long term.

By the end of this chapter you should be able to:

▶ Describe what Africa was like in the eighteenth century.
▶ Describe the part played by Africans in organising the Atlantic slave trade.
▶ Describe the impact of the Atlantic slave trade on Africa.

What was Africa like?

In 1770, most Europeans knew very little about Africa. Explorers had returned with stories of weird and scary-looking animals. Africans were described as wild, primitive people with strange rituals which often involved eating their enemies.

How accurate is the drawing of the giraffe? Why do you think explorers often exaggerated the appearance of the creatures they discovered in Africa?

Look at the drawing which is supposed to show African people. In what ways are they portrayed as being a) a bit weird and b) a bit scary?

These drawings were made in the eighteenth century, based on the stories of people who had been to Africa

11

Very few British people had actually visited Africa, but this did not stop them having strong views about the country and its inhabitants. David Hume, a famous Scottish philosopher and historian, wrote:

I … suspect the Negroes … to be naturally inferior to the whites. There never was a civilized nation of any other complexion [skin colour] than white … No ingenious manufactures [skill to make things] amongst them, no arts, no sciences.

An English journalist writing in the *Gentleman's Magazine* stated that:

The Negroes of Africa in their native country are totally incapable of refinement, arts or sciences. They are idle and lazy. The only way to civilize them is to put them to work.

Finally, a Liverpool merchant wrote in 1794:

*The people of **Bonny** are frequently at war with their neighbours, and when they take prisoners, they sacrifice them, cut them up, cook them and eat them, and drink a broth that is made of them …*

In contrast to the prejudiced and badly informed opinions of the previous three writers, this is what an English traveller wrote about the **Mandingo** people on the river Gambia:

There are three main trades among the Mandingo: ironworkers make spearheads and farming tools. They make bridles and saddles of which I have seen some very good examples, hardly to be bettered here in Britain. They have the skill to dress and dye deer skin and goat skin. A third skill is to use clay to make pots in which they cook their food.

An African writer described the African city of Timbuktu like this:

The king at his own expense employs great numbers of doctors, judges, priests and other learned men. There are manuscripts or written books, brought here from far places. For money, they use bars of gold.

Finally, this is what David Killingray, a modern historian, has said about Africa at this time:

*Across the Sahara came a new important influence to West Africa – the religion of **Islam**. Very gradually the faith brought by the trade routes was accepted. With Islam came Arabic writing and literacy, ideas about government, law and architecture.*

GLOSSARY

Bonny an area of West Africa which now includes the countries of Nigeria, Cameroon, Equatorial Guinea, São Tomé and Gabon

Mandingo a tribe of people who lived in West Africa

Islam the religion of Muslims, who believe in Muhammad and worship Allah

How would this item be made? What does the object tell us about the African who owned it?

A highly detailed ivory salt cellar made in Nigeria in the sixteenth century by a member of the Benin tribe

Was slavery new to Africa?

No, slavery was not a new thing in Africa. Thousands of years before the Atlantic slave trade, the civilisations of ancient Egypt, Greece and Rome each enslaved people from Africa.

During the Middle Ages, Arabs built an empire across northern Africa and into Europe. They enslaved people to work for them, mainly as servants in their homes. Their belief in Islam prevented them from enslaving people who shared their religion.

An ancient Roman mosaic showing enslaved African people crushing grapes to make wine

An ancient Greek sculpture of an enslaved African

During the Middle Ages, Arab traders crossed the Sahara to trade in western Africa. They brought back gold, ivory and enslaved people.

A traveller wrote this about the city of Kano:

Regular caravans of camels and horses, laden with salt, ivory, cloth and accompanied by slaves, left the city for the long journey to the markets of North Africa.

A writer called Leo Africanus wrote this description of the city of Kano in 1526:

Here … is where slaves are sold, especially upon those days when the merchants *assemble. A young slave of fifteen years of age is sold for six ducats, and children are also sold … The king of this region has a private palace where he keeps a large number of concubines and slaves.*

GLOSSARY

Merchants people who make a living from buying and selling

This picture from the Middle Ages shows Muslim traders in North Africa. They appear to be selling enslaved African people.

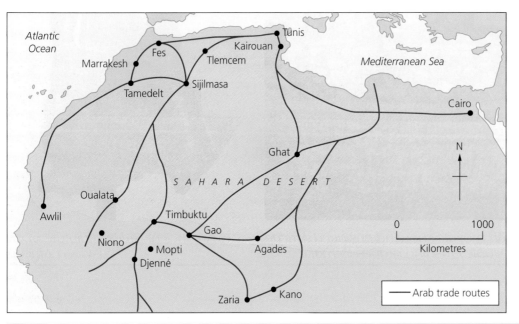

A map showing Arab trade routes across the Sahara desert linking Arab cities in North Africa with trading cities in West Africa

Try to find out what the word 'emporium' means. Why do you think this word was used to describe Kano? What do you think the group of people and animals entering the city might be?

The artist called this picture 'Kano – the Emporium of Central Africa'

How did the Atlantic slave trade start?

Portuguese explorers started to sail down the west coast of Africa from about 1540. They were looking for gold and ivory. They found Africans buying and selling slaves and started to join in with this trade.

The next step was fairly obvious and easy to make: the development of sugar plantations in the West Indies during the seventeenth and eighteenth centuries created a demand for slaves. European traders took more and more enslaved people from West Africa to the West Indies.

Portuguese traders in West Africa in the early seventeenth century, in a meeting with Queen Nzinga of Matamba

15

What part did Africans play in the Atlantic slave trade?

Although some African rulers fought against the slave trade, others were willing to supply European traders with the extra slaves they wanted.

The Asante Empire

The powerful Asante (Ashanti) people dominated the area known as the Gold Coast (now called Ghana). They had built up trade in gold with Europeans, but by the 1770s they also traded slaves. The Asante would enslave people who broke tribal laws. After 1790 they fought many wars to defend or expand their empire. Prisoners of war were often sold to the Europeans. Around a million enslaved people left the Gold Coast for the West Indies.

What was the impact of the Atlantic slave trade on Africa?

How many Africans were enslaved?

It is estimated that European ships carried 12 million people from Africa to the Americas. However, recent research suggests that about 6 million more died on the way to the coast or while they were waiting for the slave ships to arrive. Three-quarters of captives were held near the mouths of the great rivers like the Luanda, the Congo or the Niger, where killer diseases such as malaria were common.

How did the trade affect the population of Africa?

> Experts have estimated that if there had been no slave trade, the population of Africa in 1850 would have been 50 million instead of 25 million.

> Having fewer young, healthy people to produce food would make famine more likely and the death toll worse. Also, Atlantic slavery led to the movement of thousands of people across Africa, causing disease to spread and reducing the population even further.

Population

Date

How did the trade affect Africa's development?

> The movement of enslaved people and trade goods across Africa helped to improve transport networks to the coast. Atlantic slavery also led to some improvements in farming. However, this was to provide food for the slave ships rather than for feeding the local population. An awful lot of good land was left uncultivated because there were not enough young, healthy people left to farm it. The effects of the slave trade on Africa's development can still be seen today in the massive stretches of uncultivated land in fertile areas running through Ghana, Togo, Benin and Nigeria.

Did the slave trade lead to conflict between the peoples of Africa?

The slave trade encouraged conflict between tribes. Most of the enslaved Africans sold to Europeans were prisoners of war. The demand for more and more enslaved people led to increased hatred and violence between communities in Africa. Some of these conflicts are still alive today.

Did the slave trade encourage racism?

The propaganda used by supporters of the slave trade meant that racist ideas about African inferiority lasted for many years.

A cartoon published in 1902 showing British 'civilization' fighting against African 'barbarism'

Activity 1

Summarise this chapter

The following summary reminds you of what this chapter has been about. Words that are important have been made into ANAGRAMS. Your task is to sort out the anagrams and then write the correct version of this summary into your workbook or work file.

Slavery had existed in Africa since the time of the **STINGYPEA**. In the Middle Ages **BAAR** traders from North Africa started to cross the **ARASHA** desert in search of ivory, gold and slaves. In 1540, explorers from Portugal were the first **AROUSEPEN** to become involved in slave trading along the West African **TOSCA**. Over the next 250 years, over 18 million **SCANFAIR** were enslaved for the Atlantic trade. This had a disastrous effect on Africa's **UTOPIANLOP** and its **VENOMPETLED**. It increased the number of **RAWS** and led to **STARIC ITATTDUES** which continued into the twentieth century.

Activity 2

What was Africa like?

Imagine that you could have a discussion with a slave trader about life in Africa in the 1700s. Use the evidence in this chapter to produce arguments against every statement the trader makes. Copy out the statements and write your arguments on a piece of paper.

Africa is poor.
Africans are wild and uncivilised.
Africans are ignorant and uneducated.
Africans are heathens.
Africans are **cannibals**.

GLOSSARY

Cannibals people who eat human flesh or organs

Activity 3

Was slavery new to Africa?

This is how historians have described slavery in Africa before the European traders arrived.

Source A

Many societies in Africa … kept slaves. But these were mostly used for domestic purposes. They were an indication of power and wealth and not used for commercial gain.

www.bbc.co.uk (http://tinyurl.com/qsfcge)

Source B

Slavery differed from one part of Africa to another, but in most places slaves were released when they had served their master for a certain number of years, or else they could earn their freedom by good behaviour and hard work. A slave was free to marry and their children were usually born free.

Josephine Kamm, *The Slave Trade*

Source C

Africans usually enslaved 'other' people, not their own particular ethnic group. Slaves were taken as prisoners of war, in payment for debt or as a punishment for a crime.

www.discoveringbristol.org.uk

Choose five statements from the following list that can be supported by evidence from the sources above:

▶ Slavery did not exist in Africa before the Europeans arrived.
▶ Slavery had existed in Africa for thousands of years.
▶ Enslaved people were used as servants in wealthy households.
▶ A slave would have many different owners during his or her lifetime.
▶ It was unusual for someone to remain a slave for their whole life.
▶ The children of enslaved people were born free.
▶ Prisoners of war were often sold as enslaved people rather than being killed.
▶ Slavery was sometimes used as a punishment for a crime.

Activity 4

Show off your literacy skills

Edit Source A below to make it easier for your class to understand.

This is what leading historian Professor James Walvin has said about slavery in Africa.

Source A

Europeans neither invented nor created African slavery. However the entire concept and scale were transformed from the 1540s when the new sugar plantations began to encourage a different form of slave trading … The transformation of this trade from a small-scale local operation into a massive global enterprise was brought about by the rise of the sugar economy.

James Walvin, *The Slave Trade*

Try to reduce what James Walvin said to two sentences that contain his main ideas about slavery.

Activity 5

What part did Africans play in the Atlantic slave trade?

Study the picture closely. It comes from a book called *The History of Dahomey* by Archibald Dalzel, published in 1793. Archibald Dalzel worked with slave traders in Africa.

▶ What do you think is happening in the picture?
▶ In what ways is this source useful as evidence about Africa and the slave trade?

The King of Dahomey on his throne

Two well-dressed white people

An African lying down in front of the king

The King of Dahomey

This is what King Gezo of **Dahomey** said about slavery.

Source A

The slave trade is the ruling principle of my people. It is the source and the glory of their wealth ... the mother lulls the child to sleep with notes of triumph over an enemy reduced to slavery.

King Gezo of Dahomey, quoted on www.bbc.co.uk (http://tinyurl.com/qsfcge)

▶ What does Source A tell us about African attitudes to slavery?

GLOSSARY

Dahomey a country in West Africa now known as Benin

King Gezo of Dahomey

Activity 6

Further examination of Africans' role in the Atlantic slave trade?

Sources A–E were written by modern historians.

Source A

Chiefs and kings received large profits from slave trading. Chiefs could charge a tax on the export of slaves and demand fees for permission to trade ... the ruler could insist that his personal slaves were bought first, regardless of their quality ... the chief also set the final price for slaves ... The ships also had to buy their supplies of food and particularly water for the middle passage from the Africans at whatever price they cared to set.

Pip Jones, *Satan's Kingdom*

Source B

In the 18th century, Kings of Dahomey ... became big players in the slave trade, waging a bitter war on their neighbours, resulting in the capture of 10,000 [people] ... King Tegbesu made £250,000 a year selling people into slavery ... King Gezo [of Dahomey] said ... that he would do anything the British wanted him to do apart from giving up the slave trade.

www.bbc.co.uk (http://tinyurl.com/6wpl3)

Source C

Africans enslaved and sold each other. However it would be wrong to view this as Africans selling 'fellow Africans'. They were enslaving and selling people from different tribes. The concept of being African had no meaning for the people involved.

Pip Jones, *Satan's Kingdom*

Source D

Africans were discriminating purchasers of trade goods. They were fussy about colour, texture and prices. About two thirds of the goods shipped to Africa to purchase slaves consisted of good quality textiles.

Kenneth Morgan, *Slavery and the British Empire*

Source E

Europeans might have superior-fire power but that was no guarantee of safety ... Their forts looked impressive but Europeans were ultimately marooned in them ... European slave traders were unable to impose firm control in Africa itself.

James Walvin, *Atlas of Slavery*

Work with a partner. Decide whether each of the statements below is true or false. Use evidence from the sources to support your choices.

- African rulers helped Europeans to organise Atlantic slavery.
- African rulers became rich through selling enslaved people to Europeans.
- African rulers sold prisoners of war to Europeans.
- African rulers were happy to sell their own people to Europeans.
- African rulers were cheated and exploited by European slave traders.
- Europeans controlled large areas of West Africa.

Activity 7

What was the impact of slavery on Africa?

Teach a lesson

In groups of three or four, produce a lesson for the rest of your class, educating them about the effects of the Atlantic slave trade on Africa.

Negotiate with your teacher to decide how long you have to prepare this lesson.

▶ Your lesson should be presented in an organised, interesting and mature way.
▶ Planning is vital and everyone in your group must participate.
▶ Your lesson should last between five and ten minutes.
▶ Your lesson must have visual material.

Question practice

National 4

1 Describe European attitudes to Africa in the eighteenth century.

Success criteria

Write an answer that gives at least two factual points of information about European attitudes to Africa in the eighteenth century.

Source A was written by Mungo Park, a Scottish explorer, who had visited Africa in the 1790s.

SOURCE A

The slaves are secured together by putting the right leg of one and the left leg of another in the same pair of chains. They can only walk very slowly. Every four slaves are fastened together by the necks. Although some slaves managed to keep their spirits up, most seem very much depressed, and sit all day in a sort of sadness, eyes fixed upon the ground.

2 How useful is Source A as evidence of the treatment of slaves when they were captured in Africa?

Success criteria

Write an answer that explains whether you think the source is useful or not. You should support your opinion by explaining in your own words:

▶ *who* wrote the source
▶ *when* the source was written
▶ *what* the source tells us about the way slaves were treated when they were captured in Africa.

National 5

1 Explain the reasons why African leaders became involved in the Atlantic slave trade. (6 marks)

To be successful, you should try to give six different reasons, based on recall, that are relevant and accurate. The main thing to remember in an 'explain' question is to provide reasons *why* something happened. A useful tip here is to use the word 'because' in your answer. After 'because' you cannot help but write a reason for something. In this case you could write: '*One reason why African leaders became involved in the Atlantic slave trade was because they could trade slaves for manufactured goods.*' [1 mark]

You can always get an additional mark by developing a reason you give. That means you give extra detail to support the point you are making. For example, '*Europeans offered manufactured trade goods such as woven cloth.*' [1 extra mark]

Source A is from a book written by a British explorer in Africa in 1796.

SOURCE A

The African can become enslaved for various reasons. This can be the result of breaking tribal laws. However, war is of all others the most common reason. Be this as it may, it is a known fact that prisoners of war in Africa are the slaves of the conquerors; and when the weak or unsuccessful warrior begs for mercy beneath the uplifted spear of his opponent, he gives up at the same time his claim to liberty, and purchases his life at the expense of his freedom.

Adapted and amended from http://bit.ly/12mBIO9

2 Evaluate the usefulness of Source A as evidence of how Africans became enslaved. (You may want to comment on who wrote it, when they wrote it, why they wrote it, what they say and what has been missed out.) (5 marks)

With this type of question, there are three ways to gather marks.

‣ The first way is to write about *who* wrote it, *when* and *why* it was written and to explain why that information makes the source more or less useful. That is worth up to 4 marks. For example, you could write: '*This source is useful as evidence because it is written by an explorer who had visited Africa and would have witnessed the slave trade.*'

‣ The second way is to focus on what's useful IN the source, in terms of what the question is asking. That is worth up to 2 marks. You need to find two pieces of evidence from the source for 2 marks AND make a comment about how useful the evidence is. You could write: '*The source tells us that Africans became enslaved as a punishment for breaking tribal laws. This is useful evidence in explaining how Africans became enslaved.*'

‣ The third way is to write about what is *less* useful in the source. Think about what could have been included which would have made the source more helpful as evidence. This is worth up to 2 marks. For example, you could write: '*The source is less useful because it does not mention the part played by Europeans in enslaving Africans.*' It is very important to keep repeating the phrases 'this source is useful because' or 'this source is less useful because', otherwise you won't get the marks that you are aiming for.

4 Britain, the Caribbean and the slave trade

What is this chapter about?

This chapter describes how London, Bristol and Liverpool – Britain's three most important ports – involved themselves in the Atlantic slave trade. The reasons for their success in slave trading are explained and how this success affected each port is examined. The involvement of Scotland in Atlantic slavery is also considered.

By the end of this chapter you should be able to:

▶ Describe the effects of Atlantic slavery on the British ports of London, Bristol and Liverpool.
▶ Explain why these ports did so well out of Atlantic slavery.

Britain's slave ports

Many British ports shared in the wealth of the triangular trade. However, 90 per cent of the ships involved in the trade left from one of three ports: London, Bristol or Liverpool.

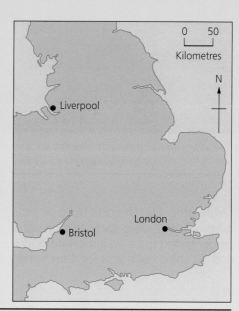

The main British ports involved in the slave trade

Date range	London	Bristol	Liverpool
1741–60	5,000	37,000	21,000
1761–70	43,000	56,000	151,000
1771–80	40,000	21,000	130,000
1781–90	31,000	31,000	155,000
1791–1800	42,000	14,000	263,000
1801–7	49,000	3,000	171,000

The number of enslaved people carried by ships from the main UK ports. Source: David Richardson, *Liverpool and Transatlantic Slavery*, Liverpool University Press, 2007, page 21.

London

From 1663 until 1698, London was the only British port that was allowed to trade in enslaved Africans. During that time, London vessels carried more than 150,000 Africans into slavery.

Can you identify two famous London landmarks?

The River Thames and London Docks in the late eighteenth century. On the right you can see the City of London.

After 1698, merchants from other British ports became more involved in Atlantic slavery. By 1730, ships from Bristol were carrying more enslaved people than London ships. However, London continued to be an important port for slave ships. During the next 75 years, around 50 ships each year left London docks for Africa to collect enslaved people.

How did the City of London benefit from the slave trade?

Although London became less important as a port for slave ships, London merchants found other ways of making money from the triangular trade.

The oldest part of London, known as **the City**, has always been involved in trade. Today, it is Britain's financial centre and home to many internationally famous banks and insurance companies. Some of the most famous City companies made their reputations by supporting the Atlantic Slave Trade.

The City of London provided the **financial services** that were necessary for the success of Atlantic slavery. From the late 1600s to the early 1800s, the demand for financial services such as insurance and long-term loans created new opportunities for making money in the City.

Slave merchants and sugar plantation owners had to be able to borrow money. A merchant needed to buy or rent a ship, fill it with trade goods and pay wages to a captain and crew before it left for Africa. He might have to wait 18 months before his ship returned; only then could he count his profits.

Merchants involved in the triangular trade also needed insurance. If their vessel hit a storm during its voyage, the **cargo** could be lost. Without insurance, a trader could lose everything.

Which of today's well-known companies made money from the slave trade?

- Lloyd's of London is a famous, long-established company with its roots in transatlantic slave trading. It started as a small business based in a London coffee house. The profits made from insuring slave ships allowed it to grow into one of the world's largest banking and insurance houses.
- David and Alexander Barclay made vast amounts of money from the transatlantic slave trade. They set up Barclays Bank in order to provide loans to other merchants.
- The Bank of England was set up in 1694. It provided finance for slave traders and plantation owners. Some of the top people in the bank also owned plantations in the West Indies.
- Sir Francis Baring is believed to have made a fortune as a 16-year-old slave dealer. He used his profits to start Barings Bank.

> ### GLOSSARY
> **The City** the important financial district of London
> **Financial services** services involving money like banking, credit and insurance
> **Cargo** the valuable contents of a trading ship

> What sort of people would you meet in a place like this? What kinds of business do you think would go on?

A coffee house in the City of London in the eighteenth century. Coffee was a luxury drink at this time.

Bristol

How did Bristol benefit from the slave trade?

Bristol had been an important trading port since the Middle Ages. Its position on the west coast of England gave it an advantage over London in the trade with the Caribbean.

Bristol merchants were not allowed to trade in enslaved African people until 1698, but there is strong evidence that they were illegally trading in enslaved people at least as early as the 1670s. From that time on, Bristol merchants, who were great entrepreneurs, increased their trade with the islands of the Caribbean. They also became specialists in trading with West Africa, marketing slaves in West Indies' colonies such as St Kitts and supplying slaves to England's largest sugar-producing island, Jamaica.

Bristol merchants developed close relationships with slave traders in West Africa. These ties survived for generations because African traders seemed to trust Bristol merchants more than those from other ports.

Bristol boomed because of its slave-trading success. Merchants spent money on fine new buildings in the centre of the city. Industries such as copper-smelting, sugar-refining and glass-making grew as a result of the slave trade.

Today, Bristol's involvement in the slave trade can be seen in a large public plaque. It recognises not only the wealth that slavery brought to Bristol, but also the shame that Bristol and other British ports now have for their involvement in the buying and selling of human beings.

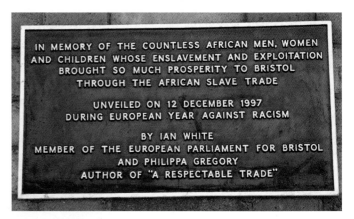

IN MEMORY OF THE COUNTLESS AFRICAN MEN, WOMEN AND CHILDREN WHOSE ENSLAVEMENT AND EXPLOITATION BROUGHT SO MUCH PROSPERITY TO BRISTOL THROUGH THE AFRICAN SLAVE TRADE

UNVEILED ON 12 DECEMBER 1997 DURING EUROPEAN YEAR AGAINST RACISM

BY IAN WHITE
MEMBER OF THE EUROPEAN PARLIAMENT FOR BRISTOL AND PHILIPPA GREGORY
AUTHOR OF "A RESPECTABLE TRADE"

A plaque displayed in Bristol, in memory of enslaved African people

Bristol docks in the eighteenth century

Liverpool

How did Liverpool benefit from the slave trade?

The first recorded slave voyage from Liverpool was by a ship called the *Liverpool Merchant* in 1700. The trip was a great success and encouraged other Liverpool merchants to become involved in the trade. In 1726, there were 21 ships in Liverpool's slave-trading fleet. By 1757, 176 Liverpool ships took part in the triangular trade. It is no exaggeration to say that the slave trade made Liverpool into one of the richest and most prosperous trading centres in the world.

By the 1780s, Liverpool had become the largest slave-ship building site in Britain, with two out of every five British vessels being built there. In the final 20 years before the slave trade was stopped, Liverpool shipbuilders constructed 469 slave ships.

The government charged a tax or duty on any trade goods entering Britain. Liverpool merchants could avoid paying taxes by importing trade goods for the triangular trade, such as foreign cloth, to the Isle of Man. The Isle of Man, close to Liverpool, was not ruled directly by Britain and did not share the same tax system as Britain (and this is still the case today). As a result, goods used to trade for slaves could be stored on the Isle of Man by Liverpool merchants until a slave ship picked them up on its way to Africa. The goods never entered Britain so no taxes could be charged on them.

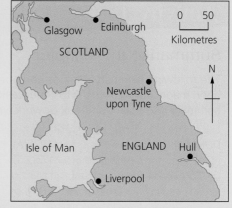

A map showing Liverpool's location

Liverpool docks in the late eighteenth century. These warehouses would store trade goods and imported sugar.

It was much cheaper to crew a slave ship from Liverpool, so traders preferred to use Liverpool as their base. Unlike London and Bristol, there were few restrictions on who could crew Liverpool ships. Young boys and inexperienced hands would be employed in preference to more experienced (and more expensive) sailors.

Liverpool's docks were also easier to use than those of Bristol or London. Liverpool had a very large, deep waterfront and was not affected by tides. Larger ships had no difficulties docking at Liverpool, so owners preferred to use the port. Ships could also be unloaded and reloaded much more quickly, which further reduced the costs of 'parking' in the docks.

As a result of all the savings that the port of Liverpool could offer, Liverpool merchants were able to sell slaves £4 or £5 cheaper than Bristol merchants. By the middle of the eighteenth century, Liverpool was sending twice as many ships to West Africa as Bristol and, by the end of the eighteenth century, Liverpool had over 60 per cent of the entire British trade.

What does this carving show? Why do these carvings appear on some Liverpool buildings?

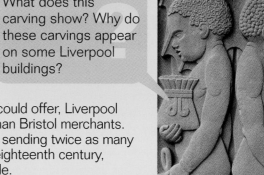

Carvings like this can still be seen on buildings in the centre of Liverpool

Activity 1

Summarise this chapter

The following summary reminds you of what this chapter has been about. Words that are important have been made into ANAGRAMS. Your task is to sort out the anagrams and then write the correct version of this summary into your workbook or work file.

London was the British port with the longest involvement in slave trading. The oldest part, known as the **TYIC FO DONLON,** provided important **NANCIFIAL RIVESCES** to slave merchants and **TALONPINTA** owners. Bristol became the most important slave port after 1730. The city was known for its **PUNTERSNEEERR** who were prepared to take the **SKIRS** needed to be successful in the triangular trade. Profits were used for fine **LIDBUGSIN** and jobs were created in industries such as **GARUS GRIFENIN.** By 1770, more ships involved in Atlantic slavery left **EVILLOPOR** than any other port in Britain. Liverpool became an important **IBLUSHPIDGIN** city because of the need for slave ships. The port was helped by its large **RAFTERTOWN,** which meant that many ships could be loaded and unloaded at a time.

Activity 2

Choose the best phrase to complete the following sentences.

1 London had an advantage in Atlantic slavery because …
   - it had a harbour for ships
   - for many years it was the only port which could trade with Africa
   - it was on the west coast of Britain
   - for many years it was the capital city of Britain.

2 The area of London famous for business and trade is called …
   - the Bank
   - the City
   - the Coffee House
   - the Village.

3 London companies that give loans or sell insurance are providing …
   - personal services
   - executive services
   - united services
   - financial services.

4 The triangular trade created a demand for loans because …
   - many items had to be sold in advance
   - slaves were cheap to buy
   - many items had to be paid for in advance
   - slave merchants were very poor.

5 People who are prepared to take risks to make profits are called …
   - entrepreneurs
   - bankers
   - insurance salesmen
   - risk takers.

6 Involvement in Atlantic slavery benefited the people of London, Bristol and Liverpool because …
   - it provided many jobs
   - profits were used to build fine houses
   - the cities grew in size
   - everyone became rich.

Activity 3

Celebrating success

Choose one of the main British slave-trading ports of London, Bristol or Liverpool.

Make a presentation to your class explaining why you think the port you have chosen deserves to be called the most important port in the history of the British slave trade.

Your presentation could be given as PowerPoint slides, a wall display or an advertising poster.

- Your presentation must be clear, interesting and eye-catching.
- You must include relevant information about your port. You could include maps, pictures and statistical data.
- You must also include key points to show why you think your chosen port deserves to be called the most important.
- A strong presentation would make clear the reasons why the other ports are not as important as your choice.

Question practice

National 4

1 In what ways did British ports benefit from the slave trade?

Success criteria

Write an answer that gives at least two factual points about the ways in which British ports benefited from the slave trade.

2 Why did Liverpool become a successful port in the 1770s?

Success criteria

Write an answer that provides at least two reasons to explain why Liverpool became a successful port in the 1770s.

National 5

1 Explain the reasons for the success of British ports involved in Atlantic slavery. (6 marks)

This is another 'explain' question. Remember, to be successful, you should try to give six different reasons, based on recall, that are relevant and accurate. The main thing to keep in mind for this sort of question is to provide reasons *why* something happened. Remember to use the word 'because' in your answer. After 'because' you cannot help but write a reason for something. In this case you could write: *'One reason why British ports were successful was because the merchants in these ports developed close ties with slave traders in Africa.'* [1 mark]

You can always get an additional mark by developing a reason you give. That means you give extra detail to support the point you are making. For example, *'Bristol merchants had gained the trust of slave traders operating on the west coast of Africa.'* [1 extra mark]

Source A is based on a letter by a merchant to a London newspaper in April 1789.

SOURCE A

The manufacture of sugar, etc. could not be carried on without the trade in enslaved Africans. Planters, merchants, and thousands of workers depend for their living on this trade with the West India Islands. I have good reason to believe that nearly one third of the trade of this kingdom depends on the African trade, directly or indirectly.

2 Evaluate the usefulness of Source A as evidence of the importance of Atlantic slavery to Britain. (You may want to comment on who wrote it, when they wrote it, why they wrote it, what they say and what has been missed out.) (5 marks)

This is another 'evaluate the usefulness' question. Remember, there are three ways to gain marks. Firstly, comment on *who* wrote it, *when* and *why* it was written. Secondly, comment on the information that is in the source. Finally, comment on anything which makes the source *less* useful, such as important information that has been left out. It is very important to keep repeating the phrases 'this source is useful because' or 'this source is less useful because', otherwise you won't get the marks that you are aiming for.

Scotland and Atlantic slavery

Scotland and Atlantic slavery is not mentioned in the National 5 course, but this raises an important question about Scotland's involvement.

What part did Scotland play in Atlantic slavery?

Professor Tom Devine is a historian with a strong interest in the history of Scotland. In his book, *To the Ends of the Earth,* he writes:

There has been a long tradition in Scotland that Glasgow and the other Scottish ports ... took little or no part in the mass transportation of Africans to the plantations of America and the West Indies ... The darker aspects of the Scottish connection with the slave trade economies have tended to be either played down or ignored ...

> Why do you think the painting may have been altered?

Professor Tom Devine

A painting of the wealthy Glasgow merchant John Glassford of Dougalston at home with his family in the Shawfield Mansion. It is thought to have been painted in about 1767. An image of an African servant can just be seen on the left of the painting. It is thought that attempts were made to hide this image.

Not guilty?

Atlantic slavery was an English trade. Slave trading was very important to the British Empire but Scotland wasn't in the empire at the time.

Scotland was independent until 1707 and was not allowed to trade with the empire. Therefore, Scotland did not take part in the growing trade with British colonies in the West Indies.

Tobacco lords

It is true that Glasgow merchants made a lot of money dealing in American tobacco, which was mainly produced by enslaved Africans. But the point is that Glasgow merchants traded in tobacco, not slaves. Besides, the tobacco trade collapsed in 1775 because of the American Wars of Independence.

Slave voyages

There were no more than 30 slave voyages from Scottish ports. Most of these left from Greenock and Port Glasgow. The number of slaves transported was fewer than 5000, compared to the 3 million carried by other British ports.

There were no slave voyages from Scotland after 1766.

Scottish enlightenment

The eighteenth century saw the start of the Scottish Enlightenment. Scots like David Hume, Francis Hutcheson and Adam Smith became world famous for writing about civilisation and human freedom. Scotland was ahead of the world when it came to human rights. How could Scots have been involved in slavery?

No such thing as slavery

In 1778, the most important court in Scotland said that slavery was banned. The Court of Session said 'the state of slavery is not recognised by the laws of this kingdom, and is inconsistent with the principles thereof'.

Guilty?

Scots in the West Indies

A leading human-rights expert, Professor Geoff Palmer, notes:

Despite what many people may say, Scotland played an important role in West Indian slavery. Many slave owners and slave masters were Scottish. Tate and Lyle are dominant names in our sugar industry. Tate was English but Lyle was Scottish. Both made their fortunes from the activities of slavery. James Wedderburn was a slaver for 27 years in Jamaica. John Newland, a renowned slave master, left the town of Bathgate for Jamaica in the 1750s and in his will he gifted money which was used to build Bathgate Academy. Dollar Academy has a similar story.

Many Caribbean people are descended from the British people that enslaved them and are therefore not only part of our heritage; they are our blood relatives and have a rightful place in our society. If you look at the Jamaican telephone directory, 60 per cent of the names are Scottish.

The online resource *Scotland and the Slave Trade* states the following:

By the late 1700s, one third of Jamaican plantations were owned by Scots. Some Scots liked to dress their slaves in their clan tartan. In 1790, the combined worth of exports and imports between the West Indies and Scotland totalled at least £50 million in today's currency.

A Scottish merchant. The scarlet cloak and cocked hat are associated with the eighteenth-century tobacco lords, a group of Glasgow traders.

Scotland's love of sweets started in the eighteenth century. Wrapped sugar loaves can be seen in the background of this painting of a Glasgow grocer's shop.

A modern historian further illustrates Scotland's involvement in slavery with this source about grocery trade in Glasgow:

Robert McNair (1703–79) built up a considerable fortune in the grocery trade … [His] grocer's shop in King Street [w]as painted bright green, with two bow windows … The McNairs also became the proprietors of the Eastern Sugar House [refinery] in the Gallowgate, which allowed them to sell a range of refined sugar products, such as candies, syrup and treacle.

In his book, *It Wasnae Us: The Truth About Glasgow and Slavery*, Dr Stephen Mullen states that:

It was common for Scottish vessels to go to West Africa via European ports such as Rotterdam to load trade goods. As a result, the subsequent destination and purpose of the journey was not recorded in customs records … The influence of Scots in the business of slavery reached far beyond the boundaries of Glasgow. They were involved in the major Atlantic ports of Liverpool, Bristol and especially London … as suppliers, financiers and independent slave traders …

Richard Oswald and Bunce Island

Richard Oswald was one of a group of Scottish merchants based in London. In the 1750s, he took ownership of Bunce Island in the mouth of the Sierra Leone River in West Africa. There he set up one of the most active slave-trading posts on the West African coast.

Oswald built a golf course on the island for the benefit of white slave traders. The caddies wore tartan uniforms.

Oswald had shares in slave ships as well as plantations in the Caribbean. His ships carried slaves from Bunce Island to plantations in the Americas. The ships then returned to England with cargoes of sugar and tobacco.

The remains of the fort on Bunce Island, Sierra Leone, can still be seen today

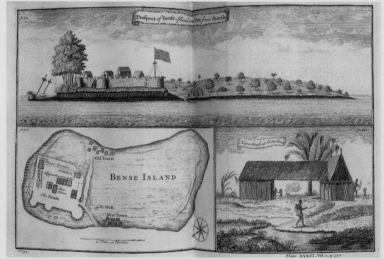

The slave fort on Bunce Island handled over 1000 enslaved people per year. A quarter of the people employed on the island were Scottish. (The drawing shows the alternative spelling of 'Bense'.)

A statue of Sir James Stirling of Keir (1740–1805) in Perth. His family owned three plantations in Jamaica.

Additional resources

▸ www.scotlandandslavery.org.uk/past1.html

▸ www.nts.org.uk/learn/downloads/Scotland%20and%20the%20SlaveTrade.pdf

Activity 4

The historian Professor Tom Devine has said: 'There was full and enthusiastic Scottish engagement at every level of the trade.'

Prepare a debate in your class on Scotland's involvement in Atlantic slavery. You could take Professor Devine's quote as the motion for the debate.

5 Merchants, profits and wealth

What is this chapter about?

This chapter describes the ways in which merchants involved in the triangular trade carried out their business and shows how they made such huge profits. It also explains the reasons why the trade benefited Britain.

By the end of this chapter you should be able to:

▶ Describe how British merchants operated.
▶ Explain why the triangular trade was so profitable.
▶ Explain why Britain benefited from trade with the Caribbean.

Thomas Leyland: slave merchant

Thomas Leyland became Liverpool's richest man. His fortune at the time of his death was more than £736,000 which would be around £70 million in today's values. He came from a humble background but he went on to become Mayor of Liverpool three times.

Leyland started his career working in the office of a small Liverpool trading company which did most of its business with Ireland. He then had a great stroke of luck: he won a large sum of money in a lottery. He used this to set himself up as a merchant and became successful by importing Spanish and Portuguese goods. From this he moved into the Atlantic slave trade.

The first ship Leyland owned, called *Lottery*, made regular voyages from Liverpool to West Africa to collect slaves who were then taken to be sold in Jamaica. The ship returned to Liverpool carrying valuable goods such as sugar. In three years, this ship alone made Thomas Leyland a profit of around £100,000.

Between 1782 and 1807, Leyland was involved in more than 70 slaving voyages. He was responsible for transporting more than 25,000 Africans into slavery.

When a law to abolish Atlantic slavery was being discussed in parliament, Leyland did everything within his power to stop it. He argued that if the slave trade was abolished, those involved in the trade would have to be paid compensation by the government.

When Atlantic slavery was abolished in 1807, Leyland started a new business. He used his great wealth to set up Leyland and Bullin's Bank in York Street, Liverpool. His business partner Richard Bullin had also made money from Atlantic slavery.

A diagram of Walton Hall. Leyland built this mansion 3 miles (5 km) north of Liverpool docks with the profits he made from the slave trade. He already owned a larger townhouse near to the city's waterfront.

Voyage of the *Enterprise*

In the summer of 1803, Thomas Leyland and three business partners invested in a slave-trading venture involving a Liverpool ship called the *Enterprise*. They employed an experienced slave ship captain named Caesar Lawson to take charge of the ship.

In an adapted extract from the ship's records, obtained from the British Online Archives, Leyland's instructions to Captain Caesar Lawson were:

You are immediately to proceed … to Bonny on the coast of Africa … You are to trade for prime Negroes, ivory and palm oil. By law this vessel is allowed to carry 400 Negroes and we request that they may all be males if possible to get them, at any rate buy as few females as in your power, because we look to a Spanish market for the disposal of your cargo where females are slow to sell.

Do not buy any above 24 years of age as it may happen that you will have to go to Jamaica where any exceeding that age would be liable to a tax of £10 per head. While the slaves are on board the ship allow them every indulgence consistent with your safety, and do not suffer any of your officers or crew to abuse or insult them in any way. Keep the vessel clean.

In the event of your death, your chief mate Mr Cowell is to take over the command of the ship and follow all our orders.

We hope you will have a happy and prosperous voyage.

The crew

Sixty-five men were hired to crew the *Enterprise* including the captain, a first mate and a **ship's surgeon**. As well as carrying 27 ordinary seamen, there were carpenters, sail makers, a gunner, an armourer, a cook and five apprentices. The total cost of employing this crew was £261.10 per month.

GLOSSARY

Ship's surgeon the person on board a ship with some medical training (on slave ships this was often very limited)

Trade goods

The following trade goods were loaded onto the *Enterprise* in Liverpool:

- Gemstones: including ten chests of mock coral, blue and black agate.
- Fine cloth: Chinese silk, English woollens, Manchester cotton.
- Firearms and explosives: including 500 Spanish muskets, four casks of shot, 230 barrels of gunpowder.
- Metals: 3500 bars of iron, 2000 bars of lead.
- Alcohol: 35 puncheons of brandy (a puncheon was about 320 litres), 312 copper-plated pint mugs and 352 half-pint mugs.
- Luxury items: including four large silk umbrellas.

The voyage

- **20 July 1803**: *Enterprise* sailed from Liverpool.
- **10 September 1803**: *Enterprise* recaptured the British ship *John of Liverpool* with 261 slaves on board. The *John* was successfully redirected to the West Indies.
- **23 September 1803**: *Enterprise* arrived at Bonny and took on board '410 Negroes' and three cases of 'elephant's teeth' (what we now call ivory).
- **6 December 1803**: sailed from Bonny.
- **9 January 1804**: arrived in Havana, Cuba. Sold 402 slaves. Ten slaves died on the ship during the voyage. Captain Lawson purchased £3800 of sugar and £233 of wood.
- **28 March 1804**: sailed from Havana.
- **26 April 1804**: arrived in Liverpool. The cargo of sugar was sold for £10,070. The wood sold for £806 and the ivory for £43.

The total profit made from the voyage of the *Enterprise* was £26,272. This would be worth over £2 million today.

Activity 1

Summarise this chapter

The following summary reminds you of what this chapter has been about. Words that are important have been made into ANAGRAMS. Your task is to sort out the anagrams and then write the correct version of this summary into your workbook or work file.

Merchants made huge profits from the **GRULIANART DRATE.** They sent ships containing **TREAD SODOG** such as cloth to West Africa, where they were exchanged for slaves who were worth much more when sold to **LAPATINTON SNEOWR** in the West Indies. This meant that the **TENCHARM** made a big **RIPTOF.** Ships then sailed from the **SWET NIDIES** with a cargo of sugar and wood and **LEPHENAT'S THETE** (ivory) from Africa. These would also be sold at a large profit back in Britain.

In this way British merchants made huge fortunes. The Liverpool merchant **SMOTHA DANEYLL** became one of the richest men in the country.

Some of the wealth was shared because merchants created **EMPTYLEMON** for others. Men were needed to load and unload the ships. Others were employed making trade goods such as **SNUG** and alcohol.

Activity 2

Which of the following words would you use to describe Thomas Leyland?

Successful	*Lucky*	*Clever*	*Racist*	*Generous*
Caring	*Respected*	*Daring*	*Sharing*	*Kind*

Support your choices with evidence.

Activity 3

The challenge! How far can you go?

Study the details of the voyage of the *Enterprise* on pages 37 and 38. The following questions go up in level of difficulty in pairs. The first two are easy. The last two are hard. How many will you try to do?

1 How many merchants shared the cost of the voyage of the *Enterprise*?
2 How many slaves was Captain Lawson told to buy?

3 What instructions did Leyland give about the treatment of the slaves on board the ship?
4 Describe the trade goods carried by the *Enterprise*.

5 Why do you think Leyland shared the costs of the voyage with other merchants?
6 Why do you think Leyland gave instructions that slaves should not be abused and the ship should be kept clean?

7 How do the crew's wages compare with the profit made by the *Enterprise*?
8 If 410 slaves boarded the *Enterprise* and ten died on the voyage, how do you explain the fact that 402 slaves were sold in the West Indies?

9 Read the log entry for 10 September 1803. In your own words, explain what you think happened on that day.
10 Why do you think the ship carried wood back from the West Indies?

Activity 4

Imagine you are a resident of Liverpool. You have read in the local newspaper that the city council wants to change the name of a road in the city.

Some city councillors want 'Leyland Road' renamed because they believe it was named after Thomas Leyland. They do not think that he deserves to be remembered by the city in this way.

Prepare a letter to the newspaper *either* supporting *or* opposing the councillors' plan. Use your knowledge of the voyage of the *Enterprise* to support your view.

Question practice

National 4

1 Describe a trading voyage on the triangular trade.

Success criteria

Write an answer that gives at least two factual points of information about trading voyages on the triangular trade.

2 Give reasons to explain why the slave trade was profitable.

Success criteria

Write an answer that provides at least two reasons to explain why the slave trade was profitable.

National 5

1 Explain the reasons why some British people supported Atlantic slavery. (6 marks)

As with previous 'explain' questions in this book, to be successful, you should try to give six different reasons, based on recall, that are relevant and accurate. The main thing to remember in this sort of question is to provide reasons *why* something happened. Remember to use the word 'because' in your answer. After 'because', you cannot help but write a reason for something. In this case, you could write: *'One reason why some British people supported Atlantic slavery was because it seemed to provide a lot of jobs.'* [1 mark]

You can always get an additional mark by developing a reason you give. That means that you give extra detail to support the point you are making. For example, *'There was work in the shipyards building slave ships.'* [1 extra mark]

Sources A and B show the attitudes of merchants towards enslaved people.

SOURCE A

Do not buy any above 24 years of age as it may happen that you will have to go to Jamaica where any exceeding that age would be liable to a tax of £10 per head. While the slaves are on board the ship allow them every indulgence consistent with your safety, and do not suffer any of your officers or crew to abuse or insult them in any way. Keep the vessel clean.

Adapted from British Online Archives records
(www.britishonlinearchives.co.uk)

SOURCE B

Merchants usually gave written instructions to their ships' captains. These often included guidance on what kind of slaves to buy. Merchants wanted young slaves as they could be sold at the highest price. Captains were expected to keep their ships as clean as possible throughout the voyage. They were often urged to look after the slaves well in order that as many as possible would survive the crossing.

2 Compare the views of Sources A and B about merchants' attitudes to slaves. (4 marks)

To be successful you must make clear whether you think the sources agree or not. There will be two 'compare the views' questions in your exam paper. In one of them, the two sources will agree on a topic and in the other question, the two sources will disagree.

For this question you would probably decide that the two sources agree, clearly outlining why you think this. That usually means you quote a brief extract from one source and another from the other source that makes a very similar point. You will get 1 mark for each comparison if you just explain in your own words in what way the sources agree or disagree with each other. If you add to your answer relevant quotes from each source that show the comparison point you have mentioned, then you will get 2 marks. Make another comparison in the same way to get the other 2 marks.

Here is an example of an answer to show you the style to aim for:

The sources agree about the attitudes of merchants to slaves. They seem to agree that merchants thought young slaves were more profitable: Source A mentions that slaves over 24 years old are 'liable to a tax' and Source B says that young slaves 'could be sold at the highest price'. The sources also agree that merchants wanted slaves to be transported in clean conditions: Source A says, 'Keep the vessel clean' and Source B says captains were expected to keep the ships 'as clean as possible throughout the voyage'.

6 Captured in Africa

What is this chapter about?

This chapter describes the ways in which some African people became enslaved and describes how they were taken to the coast to be sold to Europeans for the Atlantic slave trade. It also describes the slave factories and explains why so many Africans died before they even reached the slave ships.

By the end of this chapter you should be able to:

▸ Describe the ways in which people resisted enslavement in Africa.
▸ Explain why it was difficult for enslaved people to resist in Africa.
▸ Describe what conditions were like for enslaved people in Africa.

Enslavement

People became slaves in various ways. Many were prisoners captured in war, some were kidnapped, some had broken the law and were enslaved as a punishment. Others were sold into slavery in payment of a debt.

At first, Europeans would come ashore to kidnap as many Africans as they could find. However, they soon found that it was easier to trade with local chiefs or **middlemen**.

The African middlemen often acquired slaves many miles from the coast. Selling them on to Europeans usually meant a long, hard journey on foot. A modern source states:

> **GLOSSARY**
> **Middlemen** people employed to get slaves and sell them on to Europeans

After capture, the captives were bound together at the neck and marched barefoot hundreds of miles to the Atlantic coast. African captives typically suffered death rates of 20 per cent or more while being marched overland. Observers reported seeing hundreds of skeletons along [these routes to the coast].

This drawing shows enslaved Africans being marched to the coast

What do you think the slaves are carrying on their heads? Give at least two reasons why it would be difficult for a slave to escape on this journey.

Slave factories

An African middleman would usually sell his slaves to a European **factor** who lived on the coast. The factor often worked for a European trading company. The place where a factor worked was called a **slave factory**.

Sometimes, enslaved people were kept in large **forts**. There was a chain of 30 large stone forts along the Gold Coast of West Africa (now called Ghana). Originally they were built by Europeans to store gold. Forts like the one at Cape Coast could hold 1000 enslaved people in their cellars.

The enslaved people might be imprisoned for several months, waiting to be put on the slave ships. Conditions on the coast were very bad. Diseases like **malaria** were common at the mouths of the great rivers. It has been estimated that, in the 1770s, 45 per cent of enslaved Africans died while waiting for the slave ships.

GLOSSARY

Factor an employee of a European trading firm, who gathered slaves on the coast to supply to slave ships

Slave factories places where factors carried out their business

Forts strong stone buildings along the African coast, often used as slave factories

Malaria a deadly disease passed on by mosquito bites

A drawing of Cape Coast Castle, a British fort on the Gold Coast

Activity 1

Summarise this chapter

The following summary reminds you of what this chapter has been about. Words that are important have been made into ANAGRAMS. Your task is to sort out the anagrams and then write the correct version of this summary into your workbook or work file.

Africans could be enslaved for a number of reasons. Often they were **SPONERIRS FO AWR** taken after a battle between tribes. Sometimes they were **PINKEDPAD** during a raid by one tribe on another. Europeans would use African **LENDDIMME** to get slaves for them. By the 1770s, enslaved people were being captured deep inside Africa so they had to be **CHARMED** to the coast. They were taken to **VEALS TRISOFACE** where they were imprisoned, often in crowded and unhealthy conditions. They waited there until they could be transferred to the **ALVES HIPSS**. Many enslaved people died on the way to the coast or while waiting for the ships. Diseases like **LIARAMA** and other fevers caused many deaths on the coast.

Activity 2

Test yourself

1 Write down four ways in which an African might become enslaved.
2 What is meant by the term 'slave factory'?
3 Why do you think the death rate among enslaved people was so high in the factories?

Question practice

National 4

1 Describe the ways in which Africans could become enslaved.

Success criteria

Write an answer that gives at least two factual points of information describing the way Africans could become enslaved.

Source A is taken from evidence given by a British visitor to Africa to a Parliamentary Committee in 1789.

SOURCE A

We called at villages as we passed and purchased our slaves fairly, but in the night some of the ship's crew made several trips to the river banks and organised raiding parties. They broke into the villages and seized men, women and children.

2 How useful is Source A as evidence of the way slaves were captured?

Success criteria

Write an answer that explains whether you think the source is useful or not. You should support your opinion by explaining in your own words:

▶ *who* wrote the source
▶ *when* the source was written
▶ *what* the source tells us about the way slaves were captured.

National 5

Source A is from the autobiography of an enslaved African written in 1789.

SOURCE A

We walked for many weeks in chains. Then we saw a great river with no bank at the far side. On it lay a strange ship. We were taken to a large fort. There our African owners washed us and shaved us and rubbed our skins with palm oil to make it shine. White men came in and looked at us. After a few days the black and white traders did a deal. We were kept in the fort for several more weeks, chained and fed boiled beans till another ship arrived.

Olaudah Equiano

1 Evaluate the usefulness of Source A as evidence of the enslavement of people in Africa. (You may want to comment on who wrote it, when they wrote it, why they wrote it, what they say and what has been missed out.) (5 marks)

Remember, the three ways to gain marks here are by commenting on:

▶ *who* wrote it, *when* and *why* it was written
▶ the information that is *in* the source
▶ anything which makes the source *less* useful, such as important information that has been left out.

It is very important that you keep repeating the phrases 'this source is useful because' or 'this source is less useful because', otherwise you won't get the marks you are aiming for.

2 Describe conditions in a slave factory on the coast of West Africa. (4 marks)

As we've seen previously, successfully answered 'describe' questions require four separate, accurate points of information that are relevant to the question asked. For example, 'Slave factories were large stone buildings where hundreds of slaves would be imprisoned.' [1 mark]

If you can't remember four different points, you could write more detail about the points you can remember. For example, to develop the point about the numbers of slaves kept in a slave factory, you could write: 'Many slave factories had originally been built as secure places to store gold, so escape would be very difficult'. [1 extra mark]

7 The middle passage

What is this chapter about?

This chapter describes conditions on board the British ships on the middle passage. It describes the conditions below the decks and the daily routine of a slave ship. You will learn about the many ways in which enslaved people resisted the crew and what happened to them at the end of the middle passage.

By the end of this chapter you should be able to:

▶ Describe the ways in which people resisted enslavement on the middle passage.
▶ Explain why it was difficult for enslaved people to put up any resistance on the middle passage.
▶ Describe what conditions were like for enslaved people on the middle passage.

Boarding the slave ships

The voyage from West Africa to the West Indies became known as the middle passage.

The following sources by modern historians describe the way in which slave ships were prepared and loaded in Africa.

SOURCE 7.1

On the African coast the carpenters rigged up extra shelving below decks and constructed safety barriers and defences above … Slave ships had netting rigged around the vessel to prevent African suicides.

SOURCE 7.2

It was vital to load slaves as efficiently as possible: the longer the stay on the coast, the greater the susceptibility of slaves and crew to disease.

SOURCE 7.3

Before being taken on board, slaves often had their heads shaved and their few clothes removed. This was done to prevent disease being brought on board.

SOURCE 7.4

Africans often believed that white people had seized slaves in order to eat them … that red wine which the Europeans drank so merrily derived from blood … that the olive oil which they used so carefully came from squeezing black bodies and even the strong smelling cheese of the captain's table derived from Africans' brains.

A modern-day depiction of slaves housed in a slave ship

Why do you think the people in charge of the slaves were very nervous about this stage of the triangular trade?

This picture shows enslaved Africans being carried out to the slave ships in canoes

Conditions on board the ship

The sources below describe what life was like on a slave ship during the middle passage.

SOURCE 7.5

Slaves were chained together beneath deck, side by side … They were allowed up on deck for air and exercise for one or two hours a day.

SOURCE 7.6

We couple the sturdy men together with irons: but we allow the women and children to go freely about …

Study the picture and read the sources on this and the previous page. Imagine what the feelings of the Africans would be at this stage of their journey.

This drawing shows enslaved Africans being chained before being put in the hold of the ship

SOURCE 7.7

When the sea was rough or the weather bad, the captives were kept below for long periods and the sick and healthy remained manacled together for days on end.

SOURCE 7.8

It often happens that those who are placed at a distance from the latrine buckets, in trying to get to them, tumble over their companions, as a result of being shackled. This situation is added to by the tubs being too small and only emptied once every day.

SOURCE 7.9

On board some ships, the common sailors are allowed to have intercourse with black women if they are willing to give consent. The officers are permitted to indulge their passions among them at pleasure, and sometimes are guilty of such brutal excesses as disgrace human nature.

SOURCE 7.10

The voyage itself took between six and eight weeks. The enslaved Africans were chained together by the hand and the foot, and packed into the smallest places where there was barely enough room to lie on one's side. It was here that they ate, slept, urinated, defecated, gave birth, went insane and died. They had no idea where they were going, or what was going to happen to them.

A drawing showing enslaved Africans being exercised

Daily routine

Below are some descriptions of what would happen on board a slave ship each day. These accounts were written by people who experienced the middle passage.

SOURCE 7.11

They are fed twice a day and given a pint [about half a litre] of water. In fair weather they are allowed to come on deck at seven o' clock in the morning and to remain

there till the sun is setting. The places where they all lie are cleaned every day, some white men being appointed to do it.

SOURCE 7.12

After eight days the ship would usually be out of sight of land and the slaves would be allowed on deck … the captives would be organized in groups for the cleaning of the ship and were required to sing while doing it.

SOURCE 7.13

Rice and millet (grown in Africa) was often available. To these kidney beans, plantains, yams, potatoes, coconut, limes and oranges might be added. The food of the slaves was not much inferior either in quantity or quality to that of the crew. It was probably better than what the slaves would have had while waiting or travelling in Africa.

Disease

The captain and crew dreaded the outbreak of disease on-board. An infectious illness would spread easily through the ship.

SOURCE 7.14

*Deaths on the Middle Passage occurred largely through diseases caught in Africa … severe **gastroenteritis**, **dysentery**, **dropsy**, **scarlet fever** and **yellow fever**.*

Disease would spread most quickly if the Africans were forced to stay below deck. This is a description of what happened when a lengthy storm meant that the slaves could not come up on deck for several days.

> ### GLOSSARY
> **Gastroenteritis** severe inflammation of the stomach and intestines
>
> **Dysentery** an infection affecting the intestines causing severe diarrhoea
>
> **Dropsy** a build-up of fluid within the body, leading to swelling and pain
>
> **Scarlet fever** a disease that causes fever and a scarlet rash, spread by bacteria
>
> **Yellow fever** a tropical disease affecting the liver and kidneys, spread by a virus

SOURCE 7.15

Some wet and blowing weather having occasioned the portholes to be shut and the gratings covered, fluxes and fevers among the slaves ensued … At length their apartments became so extremely hot, as to be only sufferable for a very short time … The deck was so covered with the blood and mucus which proceeded from the consequence of the flux, that it resembled a slaughterhouse.

Crew

The following sources describe how difficult and challenging the middle passage was for a ship's crew.

SOURCE 7.16

Working on a slave ship was the most unpleasant of all deep-water sailing duties. Only the roughest and most desperate men signed up, perhaps when they were drunk or to pay off debts and sometimes out of ignorance of the conditions.

SOURCE 7.17

The sailors would sleep in hammocks or perhaps bunks slung or built into any available corner …

SOURCE 7.18

Deaths among the crew were higher on slave-trading voyages than on other oceanic crossings.

SOURCE 7.19

Sometimes the crew would be harshly treated on purpose during the 'middle passage'. Fewer hands were required on the third leg and wages could be saved if the sailors jumped ship in the West Indies. It was not uncommon to see injured sailors living rough in the Caribbean.

Life on a slave ship was so hard that few men volunteered to do the job.

SOURCE 7.20

Sometimes sailors were lured aboard slave ships by 'crimping': that is being plied with drink at an inn until penniless as well as drunk; they could be carried off as part of a bargain between innkeeper and captain.

Rebellion

The following sources show how attempts by the enslaved to take over the ship were very common.

SOURCE 7.21

I made a timely discovery today that the slaves were forming a plot for an insurrection. Surprised two of them attempting to get off their irons, and upon farther search I found some knives, stones, shot, etc., and a cold chisel. Put four boys in irons and slightly in the thumbscrews to urge them to a full confession.

SOURCE 7.22

Many deaths on slave journeys across the Atlantic derived from violence, brawls and above all rebellions. There was probably at least one insurrection every eight to ten journeys.

What do you think the slaves were trying to achieve? Why do you think rebellions on board slave ships seldom succeeded?

This drawing shows some slaves fighting with the crew of the ship

SOURCE 7.23

The African captives managed to arm themselves with various weapons. They fell in crowds on our men, upon the deck unawares, and stabbed one of the stoutest of us all. He received fourteen or fifteen wounds from their knives. Next they assaulted our boatswain, and cut one of his legs so round the bone, that he could not move, the nerves being cut through; others cut our cook's throat, and others wounded three of the sailors, and threw one of them overboard. This rebellion was violently put down. Many of the most mutinous leapt overboard and drowned themselves in the ocean.

*A print showing slave **resistance** on a British slave ship*

SOURCE 7.24

Some of these frequently rose but were prevented, others rose but were quelled, and others rose and succeeded, killing almost all of the whites. Mr Town says that enquiring of the slaves into the cause of these insurrections, he has been asked 'what business he had to carry them from their country – they had wives and children whom they wanted to be with'.

Sold

At the end of the middle passage, the slaves would be sold for the highest possible prices. People soon knew if a ship had arrived carrying Africans for sale.

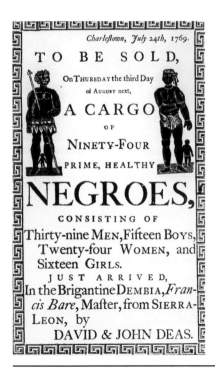

Charlestown, July 24th, 1769.

TO BE SOLD,

On THURSDAY the third Day of AUGUST next,

A CARGO

OF

NINETY-FOUR

PRIME, HEALTHY

NEGROES,

CONSISTING OF

Thirty-nine MEN, Fifteen BOYS, Twenty-four WOMEN, and Sixteen GIRLS.

JUST ARRIVED,

In the Brigantine DEMBIA, *Francis Bare*, Master, from SIERRA-LEON, by

DAVID & JOHN DEAS.

Negroes for Sale.

A Cargo of very fine stout Men and Women, in good order and fit for immediate service, just imported from the Windward Coast of Africa, in the Ship Two Brothers.— Conditions are one half Cash or Produce, the other half payable the first of January next, giving Bond and Security if required.

The Sale to be opened at 10 o'Clock each Day, in Mr. Bourdeaux's Yard, at No, 48, on the Bay.

May 19, 1784.   JOHN MITCHELL.

Thirty Seasoned Negroes

To be Sold for Credit, at Private Sale.

AMONGST which is a Carpenter, none of whom are known to be dishonest.

Also, to be sold for Cash, a regular bred young Negroe Man-Cook, born in this Country, who served several Years under an exceeding good French Cook abroad, and his Wife a middle aged Washer-Woman, (both very honest) and their two Children. Likewise, a young Man a Carpenter. For Terms apply to the Printer.

What information is given about where the slaves came from and how they can be paid for? In what ways is the sale of the 'Thirty Seasoned Negroes' different from the other two sales?

Advertisements for slave sales

SOURCE 7.25

The attention of the harbour would be caught by firing a gun, and that would attract a pilot and the visit of a doctor. The distant but all the same vile smell of vomit, sweat, stale urine and faeces wafting over the port concerned would let its citizens know that a slave ship had arrived.

Enslaved people were usually sold at an **auction**. Sometimes there would be a slave **scramble**. Enslaved people who could not be sold were known as refuse slaves.

SOURCE 7.26

The captives could be sold aboard ship, soon after it arrived or at a public auction ashore … Captives would be listed for sale by sex, approximate age and sometimes … geographical origin.

> ### GLOSSARY
> **Auction** a public sale at which 'lots' are sold to the highest bidder
> **Scramble** a public sale where buyers rush forward to claim the 'lots' they wish to buy
> **Tallies** a mark or label to aid counting

Auctioning slaves in the West Indies

A slave scramble was a very alarming experience:

SOURCE 7.27

*The people who wish for slaves are ready, when the signal is given to apply **tallies** to the slaves whom they wish to purchase by rushing all at once among them. This unexpected manoeuvre had an astonishing effect upon the slaves; they were crying out for their friends … for fear of being separated.*

The refuse slaves who no one wanted to buy, or were too ill, were often left to die unattended at the quayside of the port.

James Morley, a gunner in the 1760s, saw captives:

… lying about the beach at St Kitts, in the market place, and in different parts of the town, in a very bad condition, and apparently nobody to care for them.

Activity 1

Summarise this chapter

The following summary reminds you of what this chapter has been about. Words that are important have been made into ANAGRAMS. Your task is to sort out the anagrams and then write the correct version of this summary into your workbook or work file.

Captains of the slave ships wanted to get the enslaved people on board as quickly as possible to avoid **SEASIDE** breaking out. Nets were often rigged around the ship to prevent slave **CUEISID**. The enslaved people were forced to lie below **KECD** in the ship's hold. They were brought up for regular **RISEEXEC** and were usually fed twice a day. The main foods were rice and **ESBAN**. Common diseases to break out on board were smallpox and **TEENSYDRY**. Conditions were not much better for the **WREC** of a slave ship. They lived in constant fear of a slave **IRONBELLE**. The middle passage lasted six to eight weeks. Once the ship arrived in the West Indies, the enslaved people were **EDUCATION** or sold off in a **SCREAMLB**.

Activity 2

If this is the answer, what is the question?

Below you will find a list of words or phrases. You have to make up a question that can only be answered by the word or phrase on the list. For example, if the word 'sugar' was the answer, a question could be 'What was the expensive commodity imported into Britain from the West Indies?'

- ▷ … to prevent the enslaved people from jumping overboard
- ▷ … washed and shaved
- ▷ … they thought white people were cannibals
- ▷ … at least once a day, if the weather was good
- ▷ … kidney beans, plantains, yams, potatoes and coconut
- ▷ … scrubbing out the decks where they slept
- ▷ … six to eight weeks
- ▷ … dysentery, dropsy, scarlet fever and yellow fever
- ▷ … crimping
- ▷ … anywhere they could find to hang a hammock

Activity 3

How bad were the conditions on the middle passage?

Read Sources A–E carefully.

Source A

It was in everyone's interest to deliver as many live slaves as possible to the Americas. Brutality was neither normal nor inevitable.

Hugh Thomas, *The Slave Trade*

Source B

Before 1750, 20% of slaves died on the middle passage. However, after 1750 losses fell to 10%.

Kenneth Morgan, *Slavery and the British Empire*

Source C

In time, the men who owned [slave ships] and ran them perfected the system of loading the maximum number of Africans into a confined space, sailing across the Atlantic efficiently and speedily and delivering huge numbers of people to their destination … The crossings got faster as ship design and navigation improved.

James Walvin, *The Slave Trade*

continued ...

Source D

By 1790 many slavers were reaching the Americas without the loss of a single slave.

David Killingray, *The Transatlantic Slave Trade*

Source E

Thrice a week, we wash between the decks with buckets of vinegar ... to expel the bad air, after the place has been well scrubbed with brooms.

Captain Phillips of the slave ship *Hannibal* quoted in Hugh Thomas, *The Slave Trade*

Which of the statements below is supported by these sources? Give reasons to support your choices.

▶ The number of deaths on the middle passage had fallen by 1790.
▶ The time taken for ships to complete the middle passage became shorter and shorter.
▶ The crew did not care whether slaves survived the middle passage.
▶ Efforts were made to keep the places where the slaves lay clean.
▶ Slaves were treated brutally on the middle passage.

Activity 4

Slave resistance on the middle passage

Study the evidence on slave resistance in the extracts below.

This extract is about what happened when boarding the slave ships:

Source A

Canoes were ready to carry them off to the ship whenever the sea permitted ... When aboard ship, the men were all put in irons, shackled together, to prevent their mutiny or swimming ashore. The Negroes often leapt out of canoes, boats and ships into the sea, and kept underwater till they drowned ... They have a greater fear of Barbados than we of hell ...

Captain Thomas Phillips

This extract is about meal times:

Source B

The captain used to move about the slaves at mealtime, putting pepper and palm oil into the bowls of rice. In mid-Atlantic the slaves suddenly swarmed around him and beat out his brains with their wooden feeding bowls. The first mate ordered the crew to fire into the slaves. Eighty Negroes were shot or jumped overboard.

This extract is about life for female slaves:

Source C

Male and female slaves were kept apart by means of a strong partition at the main mast. The forepart for men, the other behind the mast is for the women ... This was because black women were often said to do whatever they could to urge their men to assert themselves and attack the crew.

Hugh Thomas, *The Slave Trade*

continued ...

This extract is about rebellion:

Source D

Through all the misery and suffering, new African identities were created ... Africans from different regions and cultures and with different languages learned to communicate with each other; many conspired to overthrow their captors together.

Edited and amended from *Recovered Histories* (www.recoveredhistories.org)

This extract is about slave suicide:

Source E

One man refused all sustenance after he came on board. Early the next morning it was found that he had attempted to cut his own throat. The ship's surgeon sewed up the wound, but the following night the man had not only torn out the sutures, but had made a similar attempt on the other side. He declared that he would never go with white men ... He died of hunger in eight or ten days.

adapted from *The Lancet*, London for 'The Abolition Project'

Work with a group. Imagine you have been employed by a company involved in Atlantic slavery. Prepare a report on 'Slave Resistance on the Middle Passage'.

▶ Describe the different types of resistance that are likely to occur.
▶ Explain when acts of resistance are most likely to take place.
▶ Explain why acts of resistance are likely on the middle passage.
▶ Produce a list of guidelines for ships' captains for avoiding incidents of slave resistance.

Activity 5

Buying enslaved people

Read this account by a plantation owner, Thomas Thistlewood and complete the task that follows.

Source A

*In regard to buying of Negroes, I would choose **men-boys and girls**, none exceeding 16 or 18 years old, as full grown men or women seldom turn out well; and besides, they shave the men so close and **gloss them over** so much that a person cannot be certain he does not buy old Negroes.*

*Have also observed that many new Negroes, who are bought fat and sleek from aboard the ship, soon fall away much in a plantation, whereas those which are **in a moderate condition** hold their flesh better and are commonly hardier.*

*On the 7th December 1761, I paid Mr John Hutt £112 for two men and £200 for one boy and three girls. The new Negroes were soon **branded** with my mark on the right shoulder.*

*Coobah: 4 foot 6 inches tall, about 15 years old. **Country name** Molia, an **Ebo**. **I put him to live** with Princess.*

Sukey: 4 foot 8 inches tall, about 14 years old. I put her to live with Job.

Maria: 4 foot 11 inches tall, about 15 years old. Country name Ogo. I put her with Lucy.

*Pompey: 4 foot 9 inches tall, about 16 years old. Country name Oworia, a **Coromante**. Put to live with Plato.*

Will: 5 foot 3 inches tall, about 22 years old. Country name Sawnno, alias Dowotronny.

'International Slavery Museum', www.liverpoolmuseums.org.uk

continued ...

Work with a partner. What do you think the author means by the following words and phrases?

- men-boys and girls
- gloss them over
- in a moderate condition

- branded
- country name
- I put him to live with

- Ebo and Coromante

Read this account by a plantation owner and complete the task that follows.

Question practice

National 4

1 Describe conditions on board a slave ship on the middle passage.

Success criteria

Write an answer that gives at least two factual points of information about conditions on board a slave ship on the middle passage.

Source A is a plan of the slave ship *Brookes*, produced by Thomas Clarkson, an opponent of the slave trade, in 1788.

SOURCE A

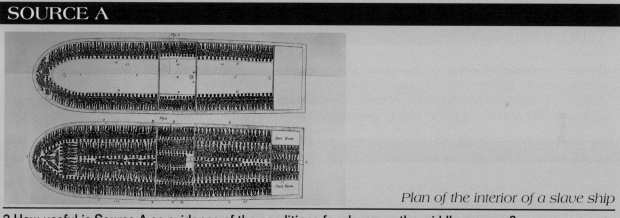

Plan of the interior of a slave ship

2 How useful is Source A as evidence of the conditions for slaves on the middle passage?

Success criteria

Write an answer that explains whether you think the source is useful or not. You should support your opinion by explaining in your own words:

- *who* produced the source
- *when* the source was produced
- *what* the source tells us about the conditions for slaves on the middle passage.

National 5

1 To what extent was the failure of resistance on the middle passage due to the poor physical state of the enslaved people? (9 marks)

'To what extent' questions always carry 9 marks, but there will be no source to help you. To be successful, you must give a short introduction that shows you understand that other factors must be considered as well as the one mentioned in the question. So, your answer could begin: *'The poor physical state of enslaved people contributed to the failure of resistance on the middle passage, but there were other factors such as their lack of weapons, lack of opportunity to resist and the crew were usually well armed.'*

You should then explain the importance of the factor mentioned in the question. Try to make at least two clear points. For example: *'Slaves on the middle passage were often poorly fed, which would mean they would not have enough energy to resist their captors. Disease spread quickly in the hold of the slave ship and would leave the slaves too sick to fight against the crew.'*

Now go on to explain the other factors that you identified in your introduction, such as: *'Slaves on the middle passage had no access to any weapons, so they could only resist the crew using their bare hands. The crew on a slave ship had firearms and other weapons which could be used to control any resistance. For much of the time they were on board, slaves were chained up in the hold of the ship so opportunities to resist were very limited.'*

Such an answer should give the five pieces of relevant information that you need.

Finally, use your own judgement to give a short conclusion explaining which factor you think was the most important, and give a reason to support your conclusion. For example: *'The poor physical state of the enslaved people made resistance on the middle passage very difficult. However, the crew on board were well armed which would make resistance very difficult even for fit and healthy slaves.'*

Sources A and B are about the conditions on a slave ship during the middle passage.

SOURCE A

The floor was covered with blood and mucus and resembled a slaughterhouse. After fifteen minutes I was so overcome by the stench and foul air that I nearly fainted. The heat was almost unbearable. The slaves' meals are meagre and consist chiefly of horse beans, boiled to a pulp and sometimes a quantity of beef or pork. The crew are often guilty of cruelty towards the slaves.

SOURCE B

I was soon put below decks. I had never smelt anything so bad in my life. Once the holds were full of people the stench became even worse. The heat of the climate made us sweat a lot. One day the crew caught some fish, ate all they could and threw the rest overboard. We were hungry and begged for food but they ignored us.

2 Compare the views given in Sources A and B as evidence of conditions on the middle passage. (4 marks)

This is another 'compare the views' question. Remember, for this type of question you must make clear whether you think the sources agree or not. You will get 1 mark for each comparison if you just explain in your own words in what way the sources agree or disagree with each other. If you add to your answer relevant quotes from each source that show the comparison point you have mentioned, then you will get 2 marks. If you can make two comparisons which are developed in this way, you will get 4 marks.

8 On the plantation

What is this chapter about?

This chapter describes the ways in which enslaved Africans resisted their masters on the plantations of the West Indies. It explains why resistance was very difficult. It also describes what it was like to work on a plantation and considers the impact of the slave trade on the Caribbean islands.

By the end of this chapter you should be able to:

▶ Describe the ways in which people resisted enslavement on the plantations.
▶ Explain why it was difficult for enslaved people to resist their owners on the plantations.
▶ Describe what conditions were like for enslaved people on the plantations.
▶ Describe the impact of the slave trade on the Caribbean islands.

Thomas Thistlewood, Westmoreland, Jamaica

Thomas Thistlewood was born in Tupholme, Lincolnshire in 1721. His father was a farmer. Thomas decided to leave England in 1750 to make a new life for himself in Jamaica. He worked as an **overseer** for Mr John Cope on Egypt plantation until 1767. He then managed to buy some land and slaves for himself. At the time of his death in 1786, Thistlewood was the owner of 34 slaves.

> **GLOSSARY**
> **Overseer** a person employed by a plantation owner to be in charge of slaves

> What is the 'sugar mill'? Compare the owner's house with the slave house.

A slave master or overseer

This painting shows a West Indies sugar plantation

Thomas Thistlewood's slaves

Phibbah

Thistlewood never married, but he had a relationship with one particular slave woman which lasted for 33 years. He called her Phibbah. She belonged to the owners of the plantation where Thistlewood had worked when he first came to Jamaica. Thistlewood and Phibbah had a son called John, who died in 1780 at the age of 20.

For much of the time, Thistlewood was able to live with Phibbah by hiring her from her master. It seems that Phibbah was the person responsible for arranging this. It was very unusual for slaves to have property, but Thistlewood allowed Phibbah to have livestock and other goods which she could buy and sell – and she was allowed to keep the money she made. In his will, Thistlewood set aside money to pay for Phibbah's freedom. She is mentioned many times in Thistlewood's diaries. The diary extracts throughout this chapter are all adapted from the book *In Miserable Slavery: Thomas Thistlewood in Jamaica 1750–1786* by Douglas Hall. Here are just a few of the entries Thistlewood made about Phibbah.

22 June 1756: Begged hard of Mrs Cope to sell Phibbah to me, but she would not.

3 July 1756: Walked with Phibbah to the Negro houses and discussed various things.

4 July 1756: I lent Phibbah my horse to ride to the Cope's plantation. I sent Mrs Cope some roses. I wish they would sell her to me. Tonight very lonely and sad again. Phibbah's being gone still fresh in my mind.

5 July 1756: Phibbah sent me dried turtle eggs, biscuits, a pineapple and some cashews. 'God bless her'. Poor girl, I pity her, she is in miserable slavery.

10 November 1767: Mr Cope gave me some stock to begin a breed with and condescended to hire me Phibbah now for £18 per year. Jimmy makes fun of Phibbah as they all do.

Thistlewood's will:

I order that my Executors … purchase the freedom of a certain Negro woman slave named Phibbah, the property of John Cope … provided that no more is required than the sum of £80 … I bequeath unto the said Phibbah my Negro slave named Bess and her child named Sam together with the future children. And £100 to purchase a piece of land for the said Phibbah wherever she may choose and that they do build thereon a dwelling house suitable to her station. If Phibbah cannot be freed I give £15 per year during her life.

Despite his long relationship with Phibbah, Thistlewood often had sex with other female slaves. He recorded these in his diary. For example:

> **GLOSSARY**
> **Branding** burning a mark into a person's skin

With Little Doll on the bench in the garden shed and gave her 2 bitts.

(A bitt is a Jamaican coin.)

Lincoln

Thistlewood gave the first African he ever bought the name Lincoln. He cost £43 (£4000 in today's money) in a sale at Hertford, Jamaica, in 1756. Thistlewood noted that Lincoln was about 16 years old and around four feet nine inches (1.45 m) tall.

Lincoln was a member of the Ebo tribe from Bonny in West Africa. Thistlewood had him **branded** on the face with his 'TT' mark (his initials).

For the 24 years during which he belonged to Thistlewood, Lincoln suffered a number of illnesses including chicken pox, dysentery, mumps, gonorrhoea and many 'fevers'. He also suffered from crab yaws, a skin disease found in the West Indies which causes painful ulcers. Lincoln had these on his hands and feet.

Thistlewood paired Lincoln with a young female slave called Violet. Later, Lincoln lived with another woman called Sukey. Eventually, he settled with Abba.

Lincoln was punished many times on Thistlewood's orders, mainly for trying to find ways of getting money. For example, he was occasionally allowed to go fishing rather than work in the fields. He was whipped many times for returning with very few fish. It took Thistlewood a long time to work out that Lincoln was catching plenty of fish but then selling most of them before returning home.

Lincoln and Thistlewood often argued. On at least one occasion, Thistlewood claimed he had knocked Lincoln to the ground in a fight.

Lincoln left the plantation without permission on at least three occasions and was once punished by having to wear an iron collar. However, Thistlewood trusted him enough to make him his **driver** for a while. This put him in charge of the enslaved people working in the fields. Once, when there was a slave revolt going on nearby, Lincoln was given a **ticket** to carry a weapon while he was guarding Thistlewood's property.

Lincoln kept alive the traditions of his homeland. He and another Ebo made a *banjar*, which is an African stringed instrument. One night, Thistlewood heard them playing music in one of the slave houses. He was furious and smashed the instrument with his sword.

> ### GLOSSARY
> **Driver** the person put in charge of a group of slaves (where the term 'slave driver' comes from)
>
> **Ticket** a piece of paper signed by a slave owner giving permission for a slave to do something

Sawnno (Dick)

Sawnno was an Ebo from Bonny purchased by Thistlewood in December 1761 for £56. He was given the name Dick and branded with Thistlewood's mark on his right shoulder. He was five feet three inches (1.60 m) tall and around 25 years old. During the 20 years that he worked for Thistlewood, he suffered from crab yaws and stomach ache but was otherwise quite healthy. He was once bitten by a blue shark when he was fishing.

In 1776, Sawnno was matched with Bess. Later, he shared a house with Mirtilla.

Sawnno worked as a field hand for nine years. During this time, there is no record of him being punished by Thistlewood. He was trusted to work as an assistant to the skilled slaves that Thistlewood hired to fix machinery or repair buildings. Thistlewood once rewarded him for reporting the theft of wood from the plantation. He was often sent to search for **runaway slaves**.

In 1781, Thistlewood made Sawnno his driver in charge of the other field hands. It was then that he started to receive more punishments. On several occasions he received a **flogging** for being too soft. He would allow field hands to skip work if they said they were unwell. On one occasion, he was flogged for not reporting that another slave was refusing to work. He was also punished for 'allowing' the slaves to plant seed potatoes upside down. As driver, Sawnno was responsible for disciplining the other slaves. He was once flogged for not whipping a slave named Jimmy hard enough. Eventually, he lost his job as driver.

After this, Sawnno became more troublesome. Thistlewood's diary records that he was once flogged along with Mirtilla for 'evil doings'.

> ### GLOSSARY
> **Runaway slaves** slaves who leave the owner's property without permission
>
> **Flogging** whipping given as a punishment

Chub

Chub was bought by Thistlewood with five others from a sailor in 1765. He was around 13 years old. There is no record of where he originally came from but he had scars on his cheek which Thistlewood believed to be the markings given to young males in some African tribes. He was often sick and suffered from boils, gonorrhoea, measles and crab yaws.

Chub worked mainly as a field hand, but Thistlewood also allowed him to watch the livestock. He was once flogged for allowing a wild horse to get among Thistlewood's own horses.

At first, he was sent to live with an older woman called Nanny. When he was 16 he was matched with Sally, a girl of a similar age. However, when the couple failed to produce any children, Chub was sent to live with an older man named Cyrus, from whom he learned to be a fisherman.

On several occasions he was punished along with Cyrus for returning late with few fish. After this, he ran away with Cyrus, but he was caught, flogged and sent back into the fields. Not long afterwards, Chub became ill with measles. Thistlewood paid for him to be bled by the doctor but he failed to recover. Thistlewood wrote in his diary:

Saturday, 21st October 1775: At night the Negroes buried poor Chub. I gave them a bottle of rum.

Jimmy

In 1765, Thistlewood bought a young African male of the Coromante tribe on the Gold Coast (now called Ghana). He named him Jimmy. Thistlewood estimated that he was about 16 years old, and he was five feet three inches (1.60 m) tall. He was branded on the left shoulder with Thistlewood's mark.

Apart from an unexpected bout of **smallpox** (Thistlewood had his slaves inoculated against the disease), Jimmy was quite healthy. He had crab yaws and was unable to work for a time. Thistlewood suspected that he had infected himself with the disease deliberately. On one occasion, he did not appear for work, claiming he was unwell. Thistlewood ordered him to take a 'dose of salts', believing that Jimmy was actually recovering from a late night of drunkenness.

Jimmy was often in trouble. Not long after coming to the plantation, he was flogged for taking Thistlewood's horse and galloping wildly around the fields. He was often flogged for drunkenness and for night-time disturbances in the slave houses with some of the female slaves. Once, during a violent argument with his owner, he said that he wasn't bothered by any of Thistlewood's threats because he did not care if he lived or died.

> **GLOSSARY**
> **Smallpox** a serious, contagious disease caused by a virus

Jimmy spent most of his days working as a field hand. Thistlewood did not seem to trust him to do anything else.

Franke

Franke was bought by Thistlewood in 1765. She was around 13 years old and had marks on her face which were probably the result of a ritual she had undergone in Africa. She was four feet nine inches (1.45 m) tall.

During her time with Thistlewood, Franke suffered from various fevers, gonorrhoea (from the age of 19) and crab yaws. When she was 18, she was bitten on her leg by a tarantula which made her seriously ill for several days. Thistlewood called out the doctor to treat her.

Franke worked as a field hand and was occasionally allowed to go fishing for crabs. Thistlewood permitted her to work in his house for a short time when one of the other house slaves was ill.

Franke was an attractive girl. On at least one occasion, male slaves fought over her, and Thistlewood had sexual relations with her on a number of occasions. Afterwards, he would sometimes give her money. He often gave her presents such as a bottle of rum at Christmas.

When she was 16, Franke was matched with Tom. They lived as a couple until Thistlewood decided to separate them. It appears that she was rarely punished. She was flogged for arguing with other slaves and once for saying she could not cut cane because she had backache. She was heavily pregnant at that time and miscarried a week later.

Bess

Bess came to Thistlewood's plantation in 1765 at the age of 11. She was a gift to Phibbah from her previous owner, Mr Cope. However, she was still branded with Thistlewood's mark.

Bess suffered from crab yaws and some form of sexually transmitted disease. Thistlewood called the doctor to treat her for this and she was flogged for not following the doctor's instructions.

Thistlewood decided to send Bess to a 'Miss Murray' to learn how to sew. She was rarely punished. Once, Thistlewood caught her playing a drum (a serious crime) but he chose to warn Phibbah about this rather than punishing Bess as he usually would.

Bess worked as a house slave. She was matched with Sawnno when she was 16. She had her first miscarriage in 1771. After this, Thistlewood chose to separate the couple and Bess slept in the kitchen while Sawnno was matched with Mirtilla. It is clear that Bess had sexual relations with Thistlewood at various times over the next ten years.

In August 1772, Bess gave birth to a boy whom Thistlewood named Bristol. It was a long, painful labour and Thistlewood noted that they were 'obliged to tie her down as she was so unruly'. In 1774, she was matched with another slave named Coffee. In 1776, Bess gave birth to another boy, but the child died within a day. In 1780, she had another boy who was given the name Sam. She suffered another miscarriage in 1782 and in 1783 she gave birth to another son, who died a week later. Another son died two days after birth in August 1786.

It seems that Bess was unpopular with the other slaves, who accused her of stealing from them a number of times. She was once flogged for attacking another slave in the nearby town of Savanna.

Abba

Thistlewood bought Abba for £46 in 1758 and sent her to work in the cookhouse. She became his chief house slave.

Abba was rarely punished by Thistlewood. Once she was flogged for not cleaning the house well enough. On another occasion she was punished for being caught in bed with Jimmy, who was not the partner that Thistlewood had chosen for her. When she was 22 she had a violent argument with another slave but was not punished. Thistlewood often gave her gifts; once she was given a reward for returning some money that he had lost. When she was taken ill, Thistlewood sent for a doctor to bleed her and on one occasion, when there was very little food for the slaves, he gave her money to go and buy some for herself and her children. Thistlewood had sexual relations with Abba many times over a long period and often gave her money afterwards.

In 1762, Abba had a daughter, thought to be **mulatto**, but Thistlewood said she was black. Her name was Mary. The following year Mary was blinded as a result of a bout of smallpox. In 1764, Abba had a son who was named Johnnie and two years later another who was given the name Neptune.

In December 1770, Abba was matched with Cudjoe. The following year her son Johnnie became seriously ill. Thistlewood gave her money and a ticket to take her son to the doctor in the nearby town of Savanna but, unfortunately, the boy died. Thistlewood noted in his diary that Abba was 'quite frantic and would hear no reason' for several days afterwards. He gave her rum and ordered a grave to be dug for the child near to Abba's house. Later, Abba gave Thistlewood some presents in return for his help.

The following year, Abba lost another child – a girl who died a week after birth. In August 1772, she had another daughter who was named Jenny.

The next year tragedy struck again when Abba's son Neptune died of 'a severe cold'. Thistlewood called this a 'great loss'.

During the next ten years Abba had seven more pregnancies: three miscarried and two died within a week of birth. She did have two more children; one named Phibbah and a boy called Ben. Throughout all this time, Abba was working in the kitchen as Thistlewood's chief domestic slave. However, she did not live in the house but shared a slave home with Lincoln, Sukey and her children. During the rainy season, Thistlewood noticed that water ran through Abba's house.

In 1785, Abba became a grandmother for the first time when her blind daughter, Mary, had a baby girl.

The previous year, Mary had had a miscarriage. Thistlewood had had sex with her when she was six months pregnant.

Thistlewood's diaries

Punishment of slaves

Thistlewood's diaries show how cruel he could be when punishing his slaves (as the below extracts demonstrate). However, there is no evidence that he was unusually violent by Jamaican standards. In fact, Thistlewood and his neighbours actually complained about new white people coming to the island for being too violent towards their slaves.

26 May 1770: Hard times – food is scarce. Derby was caught eating sugar cane. Had him well flogged and pickled and then made Hector defecate in his mouth.

*1 August 1770: Hazat ran away. Put him in the **bilboes**, both feet; gagged him; locked his hands together, rubbed him with molasses and left him out to the flies all day and to the mosquitoes all night.*

22 September 1770: Found a vast number of corn sticks pulled up by the roots and the best of the corn gone. Flogged all my field Negroes, except Phoeba, Franke, Mirtilla and Peggy whom I don't so much suspect.

6 December 1785: Dick has let his machete fall upon his foot and cut it, I suspect he did this on purpose. Had him flogged and chained to a 56 lb [25 kg] weight.

GLOSSARY

Mulatto a term used during slavery to describe a person with one white and one black parent (now offensive)

Bilboes an iron bar with sliding shackles attached that can be used to hold someone by the ankles

Part of Thistlewood's writings

Looking after the slaves

Sometimes, Thistlewood seemed to show some concern for his slaves, as seen in the further diary extracts below:

16 March 1752: Sancho found Morris sleeping with Quasheba, his wife. He came to me to complain. I advised them to part, which they did.

11 November 1752: Concerned about Old Sybil who was bitten by a spider which made her delirious …

28 February 1760: Coffee was coming over the bridge with a load of cane tops and somehow or other he let the cart jam him against the rails and tore one of his legs in a bad way. I sent Abraham for Dr Gorse who soon came and sewed up the wound.

Christmas Day 1766: Served a barrel of mackerel amongst the Negroes and also a pint of rum and some sugar to each Negro – except for the children.

5 July 1767: All last night and today, vast company with singing at the Negro houses, with Franke for the loss of her husband, Quashie. I delivered Franke a jug of rum.

4 September 1768: Received the powders, pills and physick [medicine] that I had ordered for my Negroes. Gave the 17 Negroes intended to be inoculated physick this morning.

14 July 1770: Gave my Negroes the day off as they are starving.

5 October 1770: Old Quashie died at Kirkpatrick this morning. He was very sensible and handy, also honest and trusty. He must have been between 60 and 70. Has for the most part been very healthy.

23 July 1774: Gave my Negroes plenty of cabbage and broccoli plants to plant in their grounds.

25 December 1774: Gave my Negroes 18 herrings each. Also, gave Lincoln, Dick and Abba each a bottle of rum, Cudjoe and Solon Caesar and Pompey, a bottle between them. Gave Abba 2 bits for Christmas. Gave them all tickets to allow them to go into Savanna.

Describe what the women in the picture are doing. What is the white person doing?

A drawing from about 1800 showing slaves working in a sugar mill

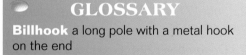

What do you think the slaves are doing? What is the job of the person in the big hat?

However, it is very difficult to find out what Thistlewood's slaves thought about him.

17 May 1760: Negroes called to work on another plantation. The Negroes one and all declare they will not move unless I go with them.

Resistance

Thistlewood complained constantly about resistance from his slaves: they were not working or doing their work badly. He was often angry at them for damaging or losing property. He punished them for being lazy, drunk or impudent and for leaving the plantation without permission.

A drawing showing slaves working the fields

*27 December 1752: Met Congo Sam who had been a runaway since the 2nd Dec. He struck at me with a **billhook** and shouted I will kill you, I will kill you! I called to Bella and Abigail but they would not assist me (Sam spoke to them in his language and I was much afraid of them). Sam was later charged and imprisoned to await trial but was acquitted. Bella and Abigail were given 100 lashes each. They then ran away.*

GLOSSARY

Billhook a long pole with a metal hook on the end

4 April 1765: Last night heard loud cheers from the Negro houses for joy that one of my Kinsmen is dead, I imagine. Strange impudence.

4 August 1766: Flogged Jimmy and Bess for meddling with my watch and telescope. Watch hour hand was bent crooked.

17 July 1767: Lucy miscarried having, I am told, drank a herbal potion lately every day on purpose. Grabbed Sancho by the curing house door, but after a struggle he slipped off his jacket and escaped. He went to Salt River but Mr Dorrill gave him a good whipping and sent him home … I punished Robert for not coming to my assistance and ordered Cyrus to be whipped for the same reason. Cyrus then ran away.

28 July 1767: Rode out to the Pen … My Negroes were not up.

29 July 1767: Went to the Pen with a whip, flogged every one of the field slaves for laziness, impudence, etc. Negroes were employed hoeing canes. Finished them in a very slight manner, not half as good as they should be.

31 July 1768: Pompey and Mr Say's Jimmy took my boat down to the sea to catch crabs, where they left her and cannot find her again.

March 1770: Sent Cyrus and Chub out fishing. They brought back about enough fish for a cat.

May 1770: Chub severely beaten for bringing no fish.

20 May 1770: Flogged Jimmy for getting drunk last night and burning a hole in my piazza floor.

24 November 1770: Jimmy and Damsel took an intolerable time to fetch water. Strapped them both.

6 June 1771: Jimmy is daily becoming more careless, stupid and ignorant through Abba's encouragement.

24 October 1771: Locked Jimmy up in the cook-room, else no resting in the night, such a noise going out and in all night long of him and the wenches.

15 November 1771: Feeling ill and very tired. At night rested very poorly. Jimmy made me a warm drink at night and an hour or two after I had been in bed thought I had been poisoned … Suspect him very much, he is very impudent, lazy, sly and sullen.

12 June 1773: My hogs get lamed and cut almost everyday, which is very surprising. Who does it and where? One hog has gone missing.

13 August 1774: My Negroes have scarce done an hour's work in the whole day so in the evening I flogged them.

Thistlewood's own Westmoreland parish was one of the areas affected by Tacky's revolt of 1760, in which at least at least 1000 local slaves took part.

May 1760, Tacky's revolt. Fifty whites killed. It was thought necessary to make a few terrible examples of some of the most guilty (three killed whites); one was condemned to be burnt. He uttered not a groan and saw his legs reduced to ashes with utmost firmness. He managed to free one of his arms, snatched a burning branch from the fire and flung it in the face of his executioner.

The impact of the slave trade on the development of the Caribbean islands

The slave trade had dramatic and long-lasting effects on the islands of the Caribbean. The native peoples of these islands, known as the Arawaks, were wiped out and replaced by West Africans who worked on the plantations. They outnumbered the white population by about 20 to 1. This created a fear of rebellion that led to the introduction of a legal system which supported slavery. The slave codes or slave laws permitted brutal punishment and even execution of slaves if they committed offences such as playing a drum, gathering after dark or carrying any weapon.

The concentration on sugar production did lasting damage to the Jamaican economy, which relied on sugar right up until the end of the nineteenth century. Any fall in the international price of sugar was disastrous for the island.

The impact of British rule during slavery has left islands like Jamaica with a sense of injustice, which is still a feature of Jamaican culture. There is a strong desire for justice and redemption for the harm done during the time of the slave trade.

Find the lyrics of 'Redemption Song' by the musician Bob Marley to discover a modern Jamaican point of view about the effects of the slave trade.

Activity 1

Summarise this chapter

The following summary reminds you of what this chapter has been about. Words that are important have been made into ANAGRAMS. Your task is to sort out the anagrams and then write the correct version of this summary into your workbook or work file.

Enslaved people found all kinds of ways of **TIGERSSIN** their owners on the plantation. They worked slowly, made deliberate mistakes and **AGEDMAD** the owner's property. They would steal when they got the chance and even try to harm the master or his friends. Enslaved people in Jamaica would often **URN YAWA**. Some enslaved people self-harmed to avoid work. Slave-owners tried to keep discipline by appointing an overseer or **REVIRD**. Enslaved people were **FOLDEGG** for the least offence. Running away from the plantation was never easy. Owners kept careful descriptions of all their slaves and usually **RENDBAD** them. Enslaved people had to carry a pass or **KICTET** if they left the plantation.

   Slaves had to grow food for themselves. They would also be given pickled fish such as herring or **KEELCRAM**. Diseases such as **OXPMALLS** and **ENTRYDYES** were common.

Activity 2

Your chance to 'free' a slave

Choose one of Thistlewood's slaves and produce a written tribute to that person.

Remember, each of these slaves was a real person. Through most of their lives they were treated as less than human. You have an opportunity to show them a little respect.

Explain what kind of person he or she was. Pick out the things you admire about the person. Comment on the things that they did during their life. You might be able to find out a little about their African background.

Activity 3

Answer these questions in full sentences.

1 Why did Thistlewood's slaves steal sugar cane and corn from him in May 1770?
2 Why might Dick have cut his own foot with a machete?
3 What gifts did Thistlewood give to his slaves? Why?
4 What steps did he take to prevent disease among his slaves? Why do you think he did this?
5 Why do you think slaves involved in Tacky's revolt were so brutally punished?

Activity 4

Work in a group. Use Thistlewood's diary and any other evidence you can find to produce a report about life on a plantation. You should make use of the following headings.

Punishment

▶ Which punishments were used?
▶ Which 'crimes' received punishment?

Looking after the slaves

▶ What evidence is there that owners cared for their slaves?
▶ What evidence is there that slaves looked to their owners for help?
▶ Why do you think owners took care of their slaves?
▶ Can you find any examples of a slave owner being nice to a slave without a selfish reason?

Resistance

Provide evidence to show that enslaved people …

▶ made a fool of their owner
▶ ignored their owner's instructions
▶ damaged their owner's property
▶ avoided giving help to their owner when he needed it

▶ hated their owner
▶ tried to harm their owner
▶ encouraged each other to resist their owner.

Question practice

National 4

Source A was written in 1787 by a former slave about the time he was sold to a plantation owner.

SOURCE A

When a signal was given the buyers rushed into the yard where the slaves were kept and the scramble began. They rushed to choose the ones they liked the best. The noise and clamour created even greater fear among the terrified Africans. In this way family and friends were separated. Most of them would never see each other again.

1 How useful is Source A as evidence about the way that slaves were sold to plantation owners?

Success criteria

Write an answer that explains whether you think the source is useful or not. You should support your opinion by explaining in your own words:

▶ *who* wrote the source
▶ *when* the source was written
▶ *what* the source tells us about the way slaves were sold to plantation owners.

2 Give reasons to explain why it was difficult for slaves to resist their owners on the plantations.

Success criteria

Write an answer that provides at least two reasons to explain why it was difficult for slaves to resist their owners on the plantations.

National 5

1 Describe the ways in which enslaved people resisted on the plantations. (4 marks)

As discussed before, to be successful in 'describe' questions, you should try to write four separate, accurate points of information that are relevant to the question asked. For example: *'Enslaved people resisted by damaging the owner's property if they were given any opportunity to do so.'* [1 mark]

If you can't remember four different points, you could write more detail about the points you can remember. For example, to develop the point about slaves damaging the owner's property, you could write: *'They would break on purpose the farming implements that they were given.'* [1 extra mark]

Source A, written by a slave, describes the hardships faced by enslaved people on a plantation in the West Indies.

SOURCE A

*The enslaved people on West Indian plantations were forced to work long hours, especially when the cane was being harvested and processed. Some tried to escape but plantation owners kept detailed descriptions of their slaves which would be publicised if one escaped, making eventual capture almost inevitable. Slaveowners would provide an occasional barrel of **salt fish** but slaves relied heavily on food which they grew for themselves. If the weather was bad their crops could fail and they would face starvation.*

2 How fully does Source A describe the hardships faced by enslaved people on the plantations? (6 marks)

Remember, to be successful in 'how fully' questions, you need to make a clearly written judgement about how fully the source explains the hardships faced by the enslaved people. In this case, you could do that by writing: 'The source partly describes the hardships faced by enslaved people, but there were other hardships not mentioned in the source.' This shows clearly that you are making a judgement.

GLOSSARY

Salt fish fish preserved with salt; a common food for enslaved people in the West Indies

You need to find at least three pieces of relevant information from the source that describe the hardships. To balance your answer, you need to write at least three extra pieces of information from your own knowledge that are relevant to the question, but which have not been mentioned in the source.

9 The abolitionists

What is this chapter about?

This chapter describes the case of the slave ship *Zong* and explains why it made many people question Atlantic slavery. It explains why the Society for the Abolition of the Slave Trade began and describes the role of early abolitionists such as Granville Sharp and Thomas Clarkson. It considers the part played by Quakers in the beginnings of the abolitionist movement.

By the end of this chapter you should be able to:

▸ Describe the case of the *Zong* and explain its importance to the abolitionist movement.
▸ Explain why the Society for the Abolition of the Slave Trade was set up.
▸ Describe the part played by Granville Sharp and Thomas Clarkson in the abolitionist campaign.

The case of the *Zong*

The *Zong* was a slave ship owned by a wealthy Liverpool merchant named William Gregson. In 1781, the ship sailed from Liverpool captained by Luke Collingwood, an experienced seaman. Gregson had insured the *Zong* for £8000. The **insurers** were the Liverpool firm Gilbert and Co.

> **GLOSSARY**
> **Insurers** people who pay the cost of an insurance claim

On 6 September 1781, the *Zong* left Cape Coast in West Africa and sailed for Jamaica with a cargo of 442 enslaved people. Captain Collingwood was ill throughout much of the voyage. For some reason, the *Zong* sailed off course and it became clear that the ship would be late in reaching Jamaica. The crew became worried that the drinking water would start to run out and some of the slaves had become ill. Collingwood came up with a plan. He gathered the crew together and warned them that if too many slaves died on board ship it was likely that the voyage would not make a profit. Then he told them, 'If the slaves were thrown alive into the sea to save the crew it would be the loss of the insurers.' The ship's first mate, Mr Kelsall, argued that, 'There is no present lack of water to justify such a measure.'

However, the crew believed Collingwood. As a result, between 29 November and 1 December, 133 sick slaves were thrown overboard to their deaths.

This picture is believed to be an illustration of the Zong massacre

Which part of the story is being shown? Who do you think might have produced this picture? Give reasons to support your answer.

The ship finally arrived in Jamaica on 22 December. Captain Luke Collingwood died shortly afterwards. The surviving 208 African captives were sold.

When the *Zong* returned to Liverpool, William Gregson demanded that the insurers pay £30 for each enslaved African who had died on the voyage. The insurers sensed that something was not quite right with the case and refused to pay. The insurers had also discovered that when the ship had arrived in Jamaica, there were still 420 gallons (1910 litres) of water on board, so the claim that it was a necessary act because of water shortage was not true. The ship's log – the written record of everything that happened on the voyage – had mysteriously disappeared.

The case came to court in March 1783 but the insurers lost. The jury saw nothing wrong in the killing of Africans to save the crew. John Lee, a senior lawyer of the time, argued that, 'Blacks are simply goods and property; it is madness to accuse these well-serving honourable men of murder. They acted out of necessity and in the most appropriate manner. To question the judgement of an experienced captain is pure folly, especially when talking of slaves. The case is the same as if horses had been thrown overboard.'

No officer or crew member was ever prosecuted for the deliberate killing of 133 enslaved people. The case did not result in a change in the law and has remained a case of insurance fraud rather than murder.

The case was widely reported in newspapers of the time. Many people were shocked by the cruelty suffered by the Africans aboard the ship. The massacre was also studied by a small but growing group of people who wanted to put an end to the cruelty of Atlantic slavery. They were known as abolitionists.

The abolitionist movement

People such as the **Quakers**, a religious group also known as the Society of Friends, had been pointing out the evils of Atlantic slavery for many years. In 1761, they had banned anyone involved in the slave trade from joining their society. The publicity created by the *Zong* case encouraged a group of young, educated men to work for the abolition of Atlantic slavery. The two most important abolitionists were **Granville Sharp** and **Thomas Clarkson**.

Sharp was a young civil servant who had lived and worked in London. He was disturbed at the way he saw Africans being treated as a result of the slave trade and tried, unsuccessfully, to have the crew of the *Zong* charged with murder. He had already fought a number of legal battles against slave owners in Britain. He had taken part in the case to free an enslaved African called James Somerset, who had escaped from his master in Britain but had been recaptured. Sharp won the case and scored an important legal victory when the Lord Chief Justice, William Mansfield, ruled that slaves could not be taken out of Britain against their will.

In 1786, Sharp met Thomas Clarkson. Clarkson was from a fairly well-off family who had sent him to study at Cambridge. There he had learned a little about Atlantic slavery and decided to try to find out more. He was shocked by what he discovered and it became his ambition to expose the evils of the trade.

Clarkson and Sharp held a meeting which led to the formation of the Society for the Abolition of the Slave Trade in 1787.

A written record of the first meeting of the Society for the Abolition of the Slave Trade on 22 May 1787

Activity 1

Summarise this chapter

The following summary reminds you of what this chapter has been about. Words that are important have been made into ANAGRAMS. Your task is to sort out the anagrams and then write the correct version of this summary into your workbook or work file.

The true horrors of the **VEALS TREAD** were kept from the people of Britain. However, in the 1770s some **TRUCO SACES** involving slavery began to attract public attention. The most important of these involved the Zong, a slave ship that sailed for **ACIAMAJ** in 1781. One hundred and thirty-three Africans were **WRONTH DROBERVOA** in what appeared to be an attempt to defraud a Liverpool **RUINSCANE** company. A London civil servant named **GRILLEVAN PARSH** tried unsuccessfully to prosecute the crew of the Zong for murder. At the court case, enslaved people were described simply as **OGRAC** which had been disposed of to save the crew. The case came to the attention of **MOTHAS NOSRALCK**, who worked with Granville Sharp to set up the **COSTIEY ROF HET LITIABOON FO TEH LAVES DREAT** in 1787.

Activity 2

The *Zong*

Pick out the true facts in the *Zong* case from this list and write them down.

- The *Zong* was owned by William Collingwood.
- A total of 442 enslaved people were loaded on board the *Zong*.
- The *Zong* was taking enslaved people to Jamaica.
- The *Zong* sailed off course because the captain fell asleep.
- Collingwood claimed that the ship was low on drinking water.
- At least 133 living enslaved people were thrown overboard.
- The ship's log showed that the *Zong* was running out of drinking water.
- The *Zong* became the subject of an insurance claim.
- Gregson was imprisoned for trying to defraud the insurance company.

Activity 3

The case for the defence

- Collingwood was an experienced captain who knew what he was doing.
- The ship's log clearly shows that the voyage was well managed.
- Unfortunately, supplies of water had run out.
- The crew opted to spare the Africans a slow, painful death.
- It was necessary to destroy the ship's cargo to save the ship.

Study the *Zong* case and the case for the defence.

Imagine you are a barrister employed by the insurers, Gilbert and Co., to prosecute the owner of the *Zong*. Prepare a speech summing up the case for the prosecution.

Activity 4

Plan a campaign

Work in a group and plan a campaign in support of a law to abolish Atlantic slavery. Remember, abolitionists faced a very difficult task. Many wealthy and powerful people supported Atlantic slavery.

You need to decide:

- the precise aim of your campaign
- the types of people you will aim your campaign at
- the methods you will use to attract support for your campaign
- how you will deal with the pro-slavery arguments.

Pro-slavery arguments

Ending the slave trade would cause lasting damage to the British economy.

Britain must remain competitive. If we stopped trading in enslaved people, our competitors in Europe would step in and take all the wealth for themselves.

Enslaved people in the West Indies have an easy time compared to hard-working British families.

Slave merchants are Britain's wealth creators. People create wealth by trading slaves and other goods. This goes into banks, which invest it in other enterprises. This creates wealth that trickles down to everyone.

British people deserve to have choice. They have the right to buy slave-produced sugar, tobacco and rum if they want to.

Question practice

National 4

1 Describe the case of the *Zong*.

Success criteria

Write an answer that gives at least two factual points of information about the case of the *Zong*.

2 Why did the abolitionist movement grow during the eighteenth century?

Success criteria

Write an answer that provides at least two reasons to explain why the abolitionist movement grew during the eighteenth century.

National 5

1 To what extent was Granville Sharp responsible for the start of the abolitionist movement? **(9 marks)**

Remember, to be successful with 'to what extent' questions, you must start with a short introduction showing that you understand that other factors must be considered, not just the one mentioned in the question.

So, your answer could begin: '*Granville Sharp helped start the abolitionist movement, but there were other factors such as the part played by the Quakers, the reaction to the case of the Zong and the important efforts of Thomas Clarkson.*'

Now explain the importance of the factor mentioned in the question. Try to make at least two clear points. Then go on to explain the other factors that you identified in your introduction. Make at least three points.

Finally, use your own judgement to give a short conclusion explaining which factor you think was the most important, and give a reason to support your conclusion.

Source A explains the growth of the abolitionist movement.

SOURCE A

The Quakers were a religious group which had opposed the slave trade since the middle of the eighteenth century. The growing demand for an end to the slave trade was encouraged by slave rebels such as Olaudah Equiano, who gave first-hand accounts of the cruelty involved in the trade. The publicity generated by the Zong case encouraged the formation of the first abolitionist society in Britain.

2 How fully does Source A explain the reasons for the growth of the abolitionist movement? **(6 marks)**

As previously discussed, 'how fully' questions need a clearly written judgement, in this case, on how fully the source explains the reasons for the growth of the abolitionist movement. For example, here you might make this judgement: '*The source partly explains the reasons for the growth of the abolitionist movement, but there were other reasons not mentioned in the source.*' This shows clearly that you are making a judgement.

You need to find at least three pieces of relevant information from the source that help to explain the growth of the abolitionist movement. For example: '*The source states that the Quakers had opposed the slave trade since the middle of the eighteenth century.*' That will gain you 1 mark. There are at least two other points you could take from the source.

Balance your answer by writing at least three extra pieces of information from your own knowledge that are relevant to the question, but which have not been mentioned in the source. For example: '*The source doesn't explain the importance of other abolitionists such as Granville Sharp.*' Try to come up with at least two other points to complete your answer.

10 The abolitionist campaign

What is this chapter about?

This chapter describes the methods used by the abolitionists to win support for their campaign. It describes the part played in this campaign by the Sons of Africa, Quakers, Evangelical Christians and women. It shows how powerful images were used to get the message across and describes the campaign inside parliament led by William Wilberforce.

By the end of this chapter you should be able to:

▶ Describe the methods used to oppose the Atlantic slave trade.
▶ Explain the reasons why the methods used by the abolitionists were effective.

The abolitionists

This is how the abolitionists organised their campaign against the slave trade.

Targeting the slave trade

The first thing the abolitionists did was to decide exactly what the aim of the campaign should be. Members of the Society for the Abolition of the Slave Trade hated slavery and wanted to see it abolished completely. However, they realised that this would raise strong opposition from the wealthy and powerful slave traders and plantation owners. They decided that the first step towards ending slavery would be to stop British ships taking enslaved people to the West Indies from Africa. They would turn to the issue of ending slavery later.

Educating people about the trade

Abolitionists saw that it would be possible to turn people against the slave trade by teaching them the truth about the cruelty involved.

Sons of Africa

In the 1780s, a small group of Africans who had managed to escape slavery formed the **Sons of Africa**. It included **Olaudah Equiano** and **Ottobah Cugoano**. They wrote about their experiences and spoke at abolitionist meetings. Equiano toured the country to promote his autobiography. Tens of thousands of people read his book or heard him speak.

In 1787, Cugoano published a book called *Thoughts and Sentiments on the Evil and Wicked Traffic of the Slavery and Commerce of the Human Species*. He argued that slavery was morally wrong and that every white man in Britain was responsible in some way for it. He wanted Britain to set an example by becoming the first country to abolish slavery completely. He argued with other important abolitionists such as **William Wilberforce** because he did not feel that enough was being done to end slavery.

GLOSSARY

Sons of Africa a group of African abolitionists that met in London during the eighteenth century

Olaudah Equiano an Ebo African who was enslaved in Barbados but bought his freedom and became an abolitionist

Ottobah Cugoano an African abolitionist who was enslaved in Grenada but became free when he was taken to London

William Wilberforce a Member of Parliament (MP) who made speeches and introduced Bills against the slave trade

Speaking tours

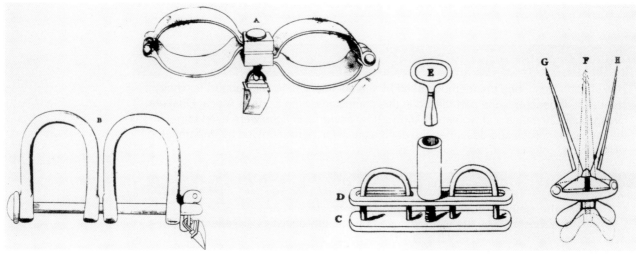

A drawing of the type of instruments Thomas Clarkson carried around in a chest with him on his speaking tours. The drawing shows shackles, thumbscrews and mouth openers.

Thomas Clarkson travelled around Britain and West Africa collecting evidence of Atlantic slavery. On his long speaking tours he would show shackles, whips and thumbscrews to his audiences. He also collected trade goods made by African craftsmen to show that there were other things besides slaves that Africa could offer for trade.

Abolitionist images

Thousands of books and pamphlets were published attacking Atlantic slavery. However, only about half of the British population could read. Therefore, it was essential to find other methods to get the message across. Campaigners realised that images could have a persuasive effect on people.

Thomas Clarkson wrote to **Josiah Wedgwood**, asking if he would help to distribute some abolitionist pamphlets. Wedgwood joined the abolitionists and asked one of the craftsmen who worked for him to design a seal for stamping the wax used to close envelopes. It showed a kneeling African in chains, lifting his hands for mercy, and included the words: 'Am I Not a Man and a Brother'.

This design became the unofficial emblem of the abolitionist movement. It appeared on pottery from Wedgwood's factory and was also used on pendants and brooches. Thomas Clarkson commented that 'fashion, which usually confines itself to worthless things, was seen promoting the cause of justice, humanity and freedom'.

How useful do you think the film would be as a source of information about the slave trade?

A scene from the 2006 film Amazing Grace. The film was made for the 200th anniversary of the abolition of the slave trade. This scene shows Thomas Clarkson played by Rufus Sewell (centre, seated).

GLOSSARY

Josiah Wedgwood a Quaker and wealthy pottery owner who supported the abolitionist movement

76

A 1796 book illustration by the famous British artist and writer William Blake. It shows a slave hung by the ribs to a gallows while still alive.

How useful is the image as a source of information about the slave trade?

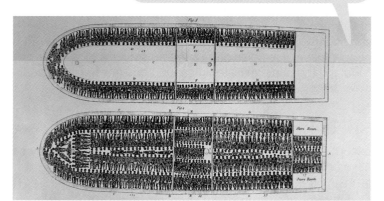

This famous image is taken from a poster produced in 1788 by an anti-slavery group from Plymouth. They took the measurements of a real Liverpool slave ship, the Brookes, and made a drawing to show how the 454 people it was licensed to carry would fit in the holds. The image was widely used by abolitionists.

The campaign in parliament

Abolitionists understood that the slave trade made some people in Britain a lot of money. The trade would never end unless it was made illegal. This would require a **Bill** to be put before parliament.

In the 1700s, only rich men could vote in Britain. Most Members of Parliament (MPs) were rich men and many owned plantations in the West Indies or had made money in the slave trade. This would make it very difficult to get a law abolishing slavery through parliament.

Petitions

Petitions against the slave trade had been sent to parliament even before the Society for the Abolition of the Slave Trade was formed. The first petition was sent in 1783 and was signed by 273 Quakers.

During 1787 and 1788, over 100 petitions containing 60,000 signatures were presented to parliament in just three months. Just about every town and city in the country organised a petition against the slave trade at one time or another.

After the first Abolition Bill was rejected in 1791, the abolitionists flooded parliament with petitions. By 1792, they had presented 519 petitions with over 390,000 signatures. This huge number seemed to show that **public opinion** was turning against Atlantic slavery.

Wedgwood's design. Josiah Wedgwood was a successful potter and businessman. Queen Charlotte appointed him the Queen's potter in 1762. He was well respected by many rich and influential people.

GLOSSARY

Bill an idea for a law

Petitions written proposals backed by a large number of signatures

Public opinion the attitude of the people

Lobbying

In the 1770s, Quakers regularly **lobbied** MPs to try to convince them of the evils of Atlantic slavery.

In 1788, Olaudah Equiano led a delegation to the House of Commons to support William Dolben's Bill to improve conditions on slave ships by limiting the number of enslaved people that a ship could carry. He also spoke to a number of MPs and the prime minister in support of a law banning the slave trade.

GLOSSARY

Lobbied tried to persuade an elected representative

Amendment a paragraph added to a Bill, usually by MPs

Speeches

Except on rare occasions, speeches to parliament can only be made by people who have been elected to serve as MPs.

In 1780, at the age of 21, William Wilberforce was elected to parliament. He was an extremely clever and witty speech-maker. In 1783, he met the influential Scottish abolitionist James Ramsay, who told him about the trade. Soon after this, Wilberforce experienced what he described as an 'intense religious conversion' which caused him to give up gambling and going to clubs.

Wilberforce began to make speeches in support of many good causes, but it was the fight against Atlantic slavery that became the most important to him.

In early 1787, he met Thomas Clarkson and a collaboration was formed lasting nearly 50 years. Clarkson collected evidence about Atlantic slavery that he gave to Wilberforce to use in his speeches to parliament.

Wilberforce made many speeches about slavery in parliament. He campaigned, on and off, for the next 18 years without success.

Bills

Wilberforce tried to get MPs to accept a Bill against the slave trade in 1789. He repeated his attempt each year from 1790 until 1806. Each time, he was fiercely opposed by those making fortunes from the trade. In 1791, MPs voted by 163 to 88 against Wilberforce's Bill. A Bill to end the trade was passed by the House of Commons in 1792 but with an **amendment** that the ban should be 'gradual', which those with an interest in the trade interpreted to mean 'never'.

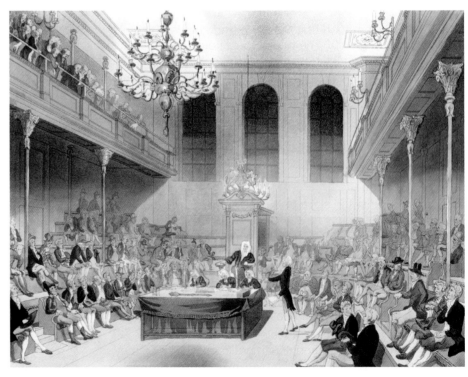

William Wilberforce speaking in the House of Commons

Christian arguments

The Church of England

Many English plantation owners and slave traders were members of the Church of England. They saw nothing wrong with slavery. They argued that slavery was mentioned many times in the Bible. The Church of England owned plantations in the West Indies which used enslaved people.

In February 2006, the Church of England's bishops voted unanimously to apologise to the descendants of the victims of slavery for its involvement in the slave trade.

Quakers

Quakers, also known as the Society of Friends, were a religious group which broke away from the main Church of England in the early seventeenth century.

The Quakers started to condemn slavery in the early 1700s. They said that it went against Christian teaching, which states that all people are equal in the sight of God. Quakers are also strongly opposed to war and they opposed Atlantic slavery because it encouraged wars in Africa.

When the Society for the Abolition of the Slave Trade was formed, there were nine Quakers among its first twelve members.

A strong organisation of Quaker communities grew up across Britain. They produced many books and pamphlets against the slave trade.

The Evangelical movement

The **Evangelical** movement grew within the Church of England in the seventeenth and eighteenth centuries. Evangelicals believed that it was important to do as Christ had taught and to treat your neighbour as you would wish to be treated. For this reason, many Evangelicals opposed Atlantic slavery. This was despite the fact that most Evangelicals still believed that black people were inferior to whites.

Some members of the Church of England were strongly against the slave trade. Most of these were also members of the Evangelical movement. These included Clarkson, Wilberforce and Sharp.

John Newton was an important Evangelical Christian who campaigned against Atlantic slavery. He had been a slave ship captain and once, while on his way to the West Indies, he became seriously ill and prayed for God to save him. He survived and this was to be a turning point in his life. In 1757, he left the trade and applied to become a priest. He admitted that he had flogged slaves and had them tortured with thumbscrews. He became Rector of St Mary's Church in London in 1779 and became a great influence over abolitionists such as William Wilberforce. In 1788, Newton published a book called *Thoughts upon the African Slave Trade*. This provided a detailed description of slave trade from the point of view of an eyewitness. He also wrote a book of hymns which included 'Amazing Grace'.

> **GLOSSARY**
>
> **Evangelical** a strict follower of the teachings of the Bible and the importance of doing the right thing
>
> **John Newton** a slave ship captain who became a church minister and an abolitionist. He wrote many hymns, including 'Amazing Grace'.

A drawing of John Newton (1725–1807) from about 1775

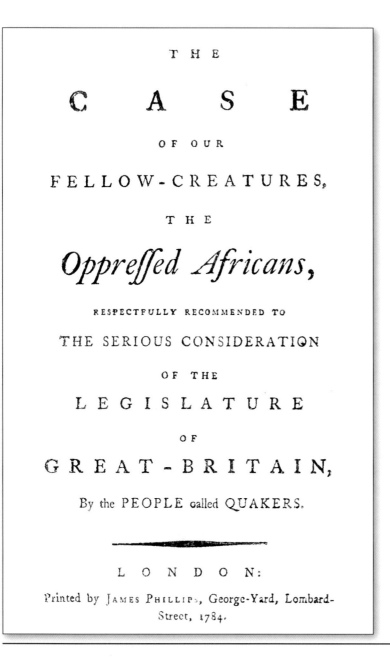

THE

C A S E

OF OUR

FELLOW-CREATURES,

THE

Oppreſſed Africans,

RESPECTFULLY RECOMMENDED TO

THE SERIOUS CONSIDERATION

OF THE

LEGISLATURE

OF

GREAT - BRITAIN,

By the PEOPLE called QUAKERS.

L O N D O N:

Printed by JAMES PHILLIPS, George-Yard, Lombard-Street, 1784.

The title page of a Quaker pamphlet from 1784

Women against Atlantic slavery

Is one half of the human species, like the poor African enslaved people, to be subject to prejudices that brutalise them only to sweeten the cup of men?

The above is a 1796 quote from Mary Wollstonecraft, a writer, abolitionist and women's rights campaigner. Another important figure in the anti-slavery movement in the 1780s and 1790s was the poet and playwright, Hannah More. She was a member of a group of Evangelicals associated with the anti-slavery campaign and a close friend of John Newton and William Wilberforce. The extract on the next page is from her 1788 poem, simply entitled *Slavery, A Poem*.

Whenever to Africa's shore I turn my eyes
Horrors of the deepest, deadliest guilt arise
I see by more than imagination shown
The burning village and the blazing town;
See the poor victim torn from social life
See the scared infant, see the shrieking wife!
See the poor wretched, dragged by
hostile hands
To distant tyrants sold in distant lands!

Many women became involved in the campaign against the slave trade, from the wealthy Georgiana, Duchess of Devonshire, to the Bristol milkmaid Ann Yearsley. However, they rarely became members of important abolitionist committees and were not invited to sign petitions. In those days, British women were treated as second-class citizens with few rights.

In 1788, the Society for the Abolition of the Slave Trade had 206 female supporters. They were mainly the wives and daughters of merchants, professionals, manufacturers and shopkeepers. They were often from Quaker or Evangelical Christian families.

Objects such as Wedgwood's cameos featuring the image of a kneeling, chained, black slave were bought by women to be used in bracelets and hairpins to publicise their support for the cause.

An earthenware jug with an anti-slavery verse

The sugar boycott

Women played a crucial role in the **sugar boycott**. This was a campaign aimed at cutting the demand for slave-produced sugar and hitting the profits of slave traders and plantation owners. In those days, buying and preparing food was seen as a woman's task. Women persuaded grocers to stop selling sugar produced by enslaved people and campaigned to get families to stop eating it.

> **GLOSSARY**
> **Sugar boycott** a campaign in the nineteenth century to stop people buying slave-produced sugar

By 1792, about 400,000 people in Britain were boycotting slave-produced sugar and grocers reported sugar sales dropping by over a third. In an advertisement in the *General Evening Post* of 6 March 1792, James Wright, a Quaker and merchant of Haverhill, Suffolk, wrote:

… I have been so moved by the suffering of our fellow creatures, the African slaves in the West India Islands … that I am taking the opportunity of informing my customers that I mean to discontinue selling the slave-produced sugar when I have disposed of the stock I have on hand, till I can obtain it through channels less contaminated, more unconnected with slavery, less polluted with human blood …

Activity 1

Summarise this chapter

The following summary reminds you of what this chapter has been about. Words that are important have been made into ANAGRAMS. Your task is to sort out the anagrams and then write the correct version of this summary into your workbook or work file.

*Most abolitionists agreed that their campaign should concentrate only on ending the **SVALE DRATE**. They were supported by some ex-slaves such as **HADUOLA NOQUIAE**. Abolitionists like Clarkson went on tours to **DUCEATE** people about Atlantic slavery. He showed images such as the famous drawing of **SELAV HIPS KROBOES**. He was helped by the wealthy businessman **SHOJIA GOWEDOWD**, who manufactured items carrying the 'Am I Not a Man and a Brother' image. The campaign against the trade in parliament was led by **MILILAW BRILFREWOCE**. He also had strong connections with members of the Christian **GILEVACELAN MEMOVENT** such as John **NEWNOT**. They had followed the example of the Quakers in opposing slavery. Women abolitionists were also active. They organised the widespread **GRUSA TOBOTYC**.*

Activity 2

Choose the best phrase to complete the following sentences.

1 The abolitionists' first aim was to end the slave trade rather than ending slavery because …
- they were not against slavery
- it was more likely to succeed
- it was what Wilberforce had planned
- they made a mistake at the first meeting.

2 The ex-slaves who campaigned against slavery were known as …
- Sons of Africa
- Sons of the Desert
- Sons of Freedom
- Sons of Slavery.

3 Ottobah Cugoano argued with Wilberforce because he didn't think Wilberforce was …
- a true abolitionist
- an MP
- serious enough about ending slavery
- a good speaker.

4 Clarkson's chest was …
- an illness of the respiratory system caused by too much travel
- a box filled with African crafts and objects used in the slave trade
- a box in which the abolitionists kept the money they had raised
- a relic of Clarkson's days as a pirate in the Caribbean.

5 Images were very important to the abolitionist campaign because …
- most people in England could not read
- most abolitionists could not read
- television had just been invented
- newspapers had just been invented.

6 The drawing of the slave ship *Brookes* was …
- the plan for the building of the first slave ship
- the main evidence used in the case of the *Zong*
- an image printed on pottery and jewellery
- a piece of abolitionist propaganda.

continued ...

7 This image was designed and marketed by ...
  ▶ Josiah Wedgwood
  ▶ William Wilberforce
  ▶ Thomas Clarkson
  ▶ John Newton.

8 A request made to parliament signed by a number of people is called ...
  ▶ a lobby
  ▶ a Bill
  ▶ a petition
  ▶ a law.

9 The MP who became well known for speaking against the slave trade in parliament was ...
  ▶ Josiah Wedgwood
  ▶ William Wilberforce
  ▶ Thomas Clarkson
  ▶ John Newton.

10 Which quote from the Bible do you think was used by Evangelical Christians to condemn slavery?
  ▶ Slaves, obey your human masters with fear and trembling, in the sincerity of your heart, as to Christ (Ephesians 6:5).
  ▶ For God so loved the world that He gave His only begotten Son (John 3:16).
  ▶ So in everything, do to others what you would have them do to you (Matthew 7:12).
  ▶ So, God created man in his own image (Genesis 1:27).

11 A Christian who believes in the importance of taking positive action to make the world a better place is ...
  ▶ a Protestant
  ▶ an Evangelical
  ▶ a Quaker
  ▶ a monk.

12 When Mary Wollstonecraft wrote: 'Is one half of the human species, like the poor African slaves, to be subject to prejudices that brutalise them only to sweeten the cup of men?', she was criticising ...
  ▶ men
  ▶ women
  ▶ slave owners
  ▶ MPs.

13 The campaign to encourage people not to buy slave-produced sugar was known as the ...
  ▶ sugar ban
  ▶ sugar boycott
  ▶ sugar blackout
  ▶ sugar rush.

Activity 3

Compare your plan for a campaign against slavery (see page 73) with the abolitionist campaign. What similarities and differences do you notice?

Question practice

National 4

1 Why was Olaudah Equiano an important figure in the abolitionist movement?

Success criteria

Write an answer that provides at least two reasons to explain why Olaudah Equiano was an important figure in the abolitionist movement.

Source A is from a speech by an abolitionist MP in 1797.

SOURCE A

Among the acts of cruelty practised daily on the plantations, an English slave driver threw a young Negro into a copper tub of boiling sugar because he said he was too sick to work. After keeping him in the tub for nearly an hour he whipped the slave severely. It took the slave nearly six months to recover.

2 How useful is Source A as evidence of the methods used by the abolitionists in their campaign against the slave trade?

Success criteria

Write an answer that explains whether you think the source is useful or not. You should support your opinion by explaining in your own words:

▶ *who* wrote the source
▶ *when* the source was written
▶ *what* the source tells us about the methods used by the abolitionists.

National 5

1 Describe the impact of the abolitionist campaign on people in Britain. (4 marks)

Remember that to be successful in 'describe' questions, you should try to write four separate, accurate points of information that are relevant to the question asked. For example: *'One impact of the campaign was that British people were shown shocking images of the slave trade.'* [1 mark]

And don't forget, if you can't remember four different points, you could write more detail about those you can remember. For example, to develop the point about abolitionist images, you might write: *'The plan of a slave ship was published to show how overcrowded they were.'* [1 extra mark]

Source A describes the methods used by the abolitionists to promote their cause.

SOURCE A

The abolitionist campaign was supported by freed slaves, such as Ottobah Cugoano, who attended meetings and spoke about their experiences. Undoubtedly, public meetings played an important part in the campaign to end the slave trade. Thomas Clarkson toured the nation describing the plight of enslaved Africans to shocked audiences. Numerous petitions were sent to parliament from cities all over the UK. The pressure on Britain's leaders became intense.

2 How fully does Source A describe the methods used by the abolitionists to promote their cause? (6 marks)

By now, you will no doubt remember that 'how fully' questions need a clearly written judgement, in this case about how fully the source describes the methods used by the abolitionists. For example: '*The source partly describes the methods used by the abolitionists, but there were other methods not mentioned in the source.*' This shows clearly that you are making a judgement.

You need to find at least three pieces of relevant information from the source that describe abolitionist methods. For example: '*The source states that freed slaves spoke at abolitionist meetings.*' That will gain you 1 mark. There are at least two other points you could take from the source.

You then need to write at least three extra pieces of information from your own knowledge that are relevant to the question, but which have not been mentioned in the source. For example: '*The sugar boycott organised by abolitionists aimed to cut the demand for slave-produced sugar.*' Try to come up with at least two other points to complete your answer.

11 Why did it take so long to end the slave trade?

What is this chapter about?

This chapter explains the reasons why it took so long to abolish the slave trade. It describes the main opposition to abolition in parliament, in the ports that benefited from the trade and in Britain generally. Events outside the country that affected the campaign, including the remarkable victories of Toussaint L'Ouverture, are also considered.

By the end of this chapter you should be able to:

▶ Describe the pro-slavery campaign against abolition.
▶ Describe opposition to abolition in British ports.
▶ Explain why it was difficult to persuade parliament to abolish the slave trade.
▶ Explain why events in Haiti delayed abolition.

Ending the slave trade

Why did the campaign to end this trade take so long to succeed?
▶ Granville Sharp brought his first legal case against slavery in 1765.
▶ The Society for the Abolition of the Slave Trade held its first protest outside parliament in 1783.
▶ William Wilberforce introduced his first Bill to abolish the slave trade in 1789.

However, in 1807 Atlantic slavery was still flourishing. Why this was the case will be considered in the following sections:
▶ the pro-slavery campaign
▶ opposition to abolition in parliament
▶ campaigns against abolition in the slave ports
▶ **Toussaint L'Ouverture** and **Haiti**.

> **GLOSSARY**
>
> **Toussaint L'Ouverture** the leader of the freed slaves in Haiti
>
> **Haiti** the first country in which slaves rose up against their masters and took over

The pro-slavery campaign

People who were making vast fortunes through owning plantations in the West Indies or trading in slaves got behind a big campaign in support of Atlantic slavery. They made speeches in support of the slave trade, for example, the below by Malachi Postlethwaite, an eighteenth-century economist:

If we have no Negroes, we can have no sugar, rum, etc. Consequently the wealth that this country gains from the importation of plantation produce will be wiped out. Hundreds of thousands of Britons making goods for the triangular trade will lose their jobs and go a begging.

They also wrote articles in magazines, such as the below which appeared in *Woodfall's Register*, 16 April 1789:

Countrymen, reflect for a moment on what you are about! – the Sugar colonies, the trade of which is more advantage to this country than most who talk about this subject are aware of, could be lost to us. The capital [wealth] from the trade is said to amount to between sixty and seventy millions, two thirds or more of which belong to the subjects [citizens] residing in this kingdom. Can England ... afford to lose so immense a sum?

Images were also published to show that enslaved people were not badly treated.

This cartoon compares a healthy, happy slave family with an unemployed, desperate British family

Opposition to abolition in parliament

Members of Parliament who supported the trade were a well-organised and powerful group. They made speeches in support of the slave trade and used delaying tactics to slow down any moves towards abolition, arguing that more time was needed to find out the truth about Atlantic slavery. Many speeches were made in parliament explaining why the slave trade should not be ended, such as this one made by Temple Luttrell on 23 May 1777:

Some gentlemen may, indeed, object to the slave trade as inhuman and evil; but let us consider that, if our colonies are to be cultivated, which can only be done by African Negroes, it is surely better to supply ourselves with those labourers in British ships, than buy them from French, Dutch or Danish traders.

> Review the information you have collected about life on the plantation. Describe three inaccuracies contained within this picture.

This illustration of plantation life was produced in 1790 by supporters of the slave trade

Supporters of slavery also gave evidence to **parliamentary inquiries** into the slave trade. Here is a description of the middle passage, given as evidence to the Parliamentary Inquiry into the Slave Trade of 1788 by James Penny, a Liverpool slave trader and plantation owner:

If the weather is sultry, and there appears the least perspiration upon their skins, when they come upon deck, there are two men attending with cloths to rub them perfectly dry, and another to give them a little cordial … they are then supplied with pipes and tobacco … They are amused with instruments of music peculiar to their own country … and when tired of music and dancing, they then go to games of chance.

On 2 April 1792, when Wilberforce again brought a Bill calling for abolition, Henry Dundas, an important member of the government, proposed a compromise solution of **gradual abolition** to take place slowly over a number of years.

Campaigns against abolition in the slave ports

People from towns like Bristol and Liverpool which benefited from Atlantic slavery campaigned against abolition in various ways. As Mayor of Liverpool, Thomas Leyland lobbied parliament to avoid abolition, claiming that it would do serious harm to the city:

The abolition of the slave trade would destroy the prosperity and possibly the existence of the West Indies, while Bristol itself, one of the most prosperous towns in England, would lose 60 per cent of its trade. In Bristol, the trades of salt herrings for consumption in the West Indies, shipbuilding, ship repairing, rope making, sail making and iron forging will be destroyed. The ending of new supplies of slaves would end sugar growing and our sugar refineries would have to be abandoned.

> ## GLOSSARY
> **Parliamentary inquiries** meetings of MPs with the aim of finding out more about an issue to report back to parliament
>
> **Gradual abolition** getting rid of the slave trade slowly

Toussaint L'Ouverture and Haiti

Events outside Britain played a part in preventing the abolition of Atlantic slavery. In the **French Revolution** of 1789, the people of France overthrew their king. Four years later, they executed him. Wealthy and powerful people in Britain were shocked by these events. Shock turned to panic when slaves on the French colony of Saint-Domingue also rose up against their rulers and ended slavery. Under the leadership of Toussaint L'Ouverture, they set up an independent country which they called Haiti.

> ## GLOSSARY
>
> **French Revolution** the uprising of the French people against their king
>
> **Slave rebellions** where many enslaved people rose up against their masters

British leaders were worried that similar **slave rebellions** might break out on neighbouring British islands such as Jamaica. They banned any moves towards abolishing the slave trade, claiming it would encourage slaves in the West Indies to revolt.

A drawing of Toussaint L'Ouverture, 1743–1803, leader of the Haitian independence movement

Activity 1

Summarise this chapter

The following summary reminds you of what this chapter has been about. Words that are important have been made into ANAGRAMS. Your task is to sort out the anagrams and then write the correct version of this summary into your workbook or work file.

The abolitionists fought hard for their cause but they faced a strong opposition in the form of a **SLO-VARPERY GAPMACIN**. Although they were only worried about their own fortunes, supporters of slavery claimed that abolition would harm the wealth and **SBOJ** of others. They claimed that slaves were actually well treated.

Most **BREMEMS FO TRAPILEMAN** supported the slave trade and spoke against all attempts to have it abolished. Some accepted gradual abolition. Some gave evidence in support of slavery to parliamentary **SQUIREINI**.

The **SOARMY** and councillors of cities which benefited from the slave trade like **PLOVEROIL** and **RIBSLOT** also attacked abolition.

Events outside Britain also made abolition difficult. The **CHREFN VELUTIROON** led to a fear of change and the overthrow of slavery in **ATIME-UNDOINGS** caused panic among Britain's leaders, who put an end to all talk of **OBTAINOIL**.

Activity 2

Match the missing words 1–6 with the words a–f below.

There were four main obstacles to abolition. Wealthy and powerful people [1] and paid for a campaign against abolition. Most MPs were supporters of slavery and used a number of different [2] to prevent any [3] in favour of abolition. The slave merchants in [4] that benefited most from Atlantic slavery were able to stir up their inhabitants against abolition. Events in France and [5] were reported in a way that made people fear any kind of change, including [6].

a supported
b Bill
c cities
d Haiti
e abolition
f tactics

Activity 3

Design a revision mobile

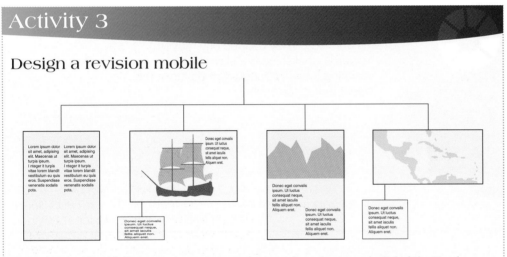

Your mobile should illustrate the reasons why it took so long to abolish Atlantic slavery. You can choose to work on your own or as part of a group no bigger than four.

If you work in a group, you must also design and use a creativity log in which you record exactly what each person in the group contributed to the final mobile.

Here are your success criteria:

▶ Your mobile must have at least four strands.
▶ Each strand should illustrate a reason why the abolition of the slave trade took so long.
▶ Each strand should have several mobile items attached.
▶ Each strand must have two text items.
▶ Each strand must have at least one large, double-sided illustration linked to an event or a person.
▶ Your mobile should hang easily.
▶ Your mobile must be clearly seen and readable from a distance.
▶ Your mobile must be attractive, colourful and relevant to the project task.

Question practice

National 4

1 Give reasons to explain why many people in Britain opposed the abolitionists.

Success criteria

Write an answer that provides at least two reasons to explain why people in Britain opposed the abolitionists.

Source A is part of a speech in parliament given by an MP defending the slave trade in 1777.

SOURCE A

Trading in human beings may seem barbarous and inhuman. However, this trade serves many benefits to the nation which outweigh all the real or imaginary bad things which are reported to have happened.

2 How useful is Source A as evidence of the difficulties in abolishing the slave trade?

Success criteria

Write an answer that explains whether you think the source is useful or not. You should support your opinion by explaining in your own words:

‣ *who* gave the speech
‣ *when* the speech was made
‣ *what* the source tells us about the difficulties in abolishing the slave trade.

National 5

Source A is about the problems faced by the abolitionists.

SOURCE A

News of the revolution in France made many British people fearful of sudden change, which harmed the abolitionist campaign. Events on the island of Haiti, where slaves killed hundreds of British soldiers, added to these fears. All this time the mayors and town councils of the ports which benefited most from the trade kept up pressure to stop abolition in its tracks.

1 How fully does Source A explain the problems faced by the abolitionist campaign? (6 marks)

Don't forget, to be successful in 'how fully' questions, you need to:

‣ make a judgement
‣ find at least three pieces of relevant information from the source, in this case, that describe abolitionist methods
‣ balance your answer by writing at least three extra pieces of information, relevant to the question, that are *not* mentioned in the source, but which are from your own knowledge instead.

2 Explain the reasons why people opposed abolition. (6 marks)

Refer to previous 'explain' questions in this book for fuller guidance on how to answer this type of question. Don't forget, to be successful you must try to give six different reasons, based on recall, that are relevant and accurate. A useful tip is to use 'because' in your answer, as you cannot help but write a reason after 'because'. For example: *'One reason why people opposed abolition was because they were influenced by anti-abolition propaganda.'* [1 mark]

Additional marks can be gained by developing your points – that means giving extra details to support the points you make. So here, you might write: *'Anti-abolition propaganda claimed that slaves were better off than most British working-class families.'* [1 extra mark]

12 Why was the slave trade abolished?

What is this chapter about?

This chapter explains the different reasons given for the abolition of the slave trade in 1807 within the British Empire. It weighs up the importance of Wilberforce's campaign in parliament and the wider abolitionist campaign throughout Britain. Economic reasons for the end of Atlantic slavery and the effects of slave rebellions in the Caribbean are also explained.

By the end of this chapter you should be able to:

▸ Explain the reasons for the abolition of the slave trade in 1807.

Wilberforce

The slave trade was ended by an Act of parliament passed in 1807. William Wilberforce is often described as the man who did most for the abolitionist movement. He tried to persuade MPs to accept the need to end the trade. If it had not been for his tireless campaign for over 20 years, it is unlikely that abolition would have taken place in the way that it did.

The 2006 film Amazing Grace *helped to mark the bicentenary of the abolition of the slave trade. This photo shows actor Ioan Gruffudd (standing) making a speech as Wilberforce.*

Abolitionists

Although Wilberforce was a tireless campaigner who introduced many Bills into parliament, they all failed. The death of Wilberforce's friend **William Pitt** in 1806 and his replacement by a new government was very important in bringing about abolition. The new prime minister, **Lord Grenville**, and the other MPs elected in 1806 had been persuaded that the time was right to end the slave trade. The actions of abolitionists like Granville Sharp, Thomas Clarkson, Olaudah Equiano and others turned public opinion against the trade. Most MPs feared losing their seat if they did not go along with the idea of abolition.

Economic arguments

Some people say that Atlantic slavery was ended because it simply was not as profitable as it had once been. Sugar production in the West Indies was never an easy business. The enslaved people were always finding ways to resist the plantation owners, and there were natural disasters such as hurricanes or outbreaks of disease that affected production. Sugar could now be produced more cheaply elsewhere, in **India** for example, without the use of enslaved people. Also, the **Industrial Revolution** had led to the development of new businesses which offered less risky ways of making profits.

An oil painting from about 1760, thought to be of Olaudah Equiano

GLOSSARY

William Pitt the British prime minister between 1783 and 1801 and again from 1804 until his death in 1806

Lord Grenville the British prime minister at the time of the abolition of the slave trade in 1807

India a country in the British Empire that produced sugar without the use of slaves

Industrial Revolution the rapid development of industry that took place in Britain in the late-eighteenth and nineteenth centuries

A drawing of an early nineteenth-century Indian sugar plantation. Sugar production in India was more efficient and did not need enslaved people.

An early nineteenth-century British coal mine and worker. The development of industry in Britain opened up less risky investment opportunities.

Slave rebellion

Slave rebellions were quite common on the British islands of the West Indies. Rumours about what had happened on Haiti (see page 89) encouraged enslaved people to be even more determined and violent. By 1806, complaints from fearful plantation owners about the stubbornness and hostility of their slaves had increased. The actions of the enslaved people themselves played an important part in bringing an end to slavery.

Activity 1

Summarise this chapter

The following summary reminds you of what this chapter has been about. Words that are important have been made into ANAGRAMS. Your task is to sort out the anagrams and then write the correct version of this summary into your workbook or work file.

William Wilberforce takes some credit for the Bill to abolish the slave trade. He campaigned in parliament for nearly **YTEWNT** years. However, the death of **ALIMWIL TIP** was an important event because the new prime minister was more committed to abolition. By this time, the abolitionists had been successful in swinging **BLIPCU PIONION** behind their campaign.

Economic factors also helped. Slavery was less **BAITERFLOP** than free labour. The growth of new industries such as **LOCA GINNIM** offered wealthy people less risky businesses in which to **VETSIN**.

SALVE BRILLEONES caused fear and alarm and played an important part in convincing some people that the time for change had come.

Activity 2

The 'in your own words' challenge

Below you will see a list of expert opinions about why Atlantic slavery ended. The views get more complicated the further down the list you go. Try to explain each view in your own words and state whether or not you agree with it. See how far down the list you can get!

Expert 1

British prosperity no longer relied on slave labour since domestic industries such as coal, iron and textiles had developed rapidly.

Tom Monaghan, author and History teacher

Expert 2

Wilberforce and his supporters introduced many Bills to end the slave trade, but they were all defeated. It wasn't until 1806 that the general climate of opinion seemed to be changing. The British Caribbean colonies were ... becoming less important to Britain as sugar producers. Merchants had found that they could buy sugar from Cuba and Brazil at lower prices.

Rosemary Rees, author and History examiner

Expert 3

[The] British Abolition Society campaigned locally against the trade among all classes of society and bombarded parliament with petitions signed by tens of thousands of people. The growing awareness of African resistance to their sufferings, both on ships and on the plantations, persuaded more people to support the campaign ... It was becoming clear beyond dispute that Africans hated their bondage and wanted it to end.

James Walvin, Professor of History, University of York

Expert 4

Starting in the 1760s, the demand to end the slave trade grew into a major political pressure group. But perhaps of equal importance was the steady change in Britain's economy towards industrial production ... The West Indian sugar-producing islands steadily declined in importance as Britain expanded her trade with Asia.

David Killingray, Professor of History, University of London

continued ...

Expert 5

Those who see in abolition the gradually awakened conscience of mankind should ask themselves why it is that man's conscience, which had slept peacefully for so many centuries, should suddenly awaken just at the time when men began to see the unprofitableness of slavery as a method of production in the West Indian colonies.

CLR James, writer and historian

Expert 6

In August 1791 a slave rebellion broke out and ... in 1804 the republic of Haiti was declared. I don't think there is any doubt that this was a huge event for the whole Atlantic world. It helped persuade Britain's leaders that it might be prudent [wise] to suppress [end] the slave trade. A pamphlet by Lord Brougham in 1804 said it was crazy to import new African captives into such an unstable situation as the Caribbean. This was throwing fuel on the flames, he said, and it would be better to stop the Atlantic slave trade.

Robin Blackburn, Professor of Sociology, University of Essex

Question practice

National 4

1 Describe the part played by William Wilberforce in bringing about the end of the slave trade.

Success criteria

Write an answer that gives at least two factual points of information describing the part played by William Wilberforce in bringing about the end of the slave trade.

2 Why was the slave trade abolished in 1807?

Success criteria

Write an answer that provides at least two reasons to explain why the slave trade was abolished in 1807.

National 5

1 Explain the reasons why many people supported abolition by 1807. (6 marks)

As with other 'explain' questions described in this book, you should aim to include six relevant and accurate reasons from recall to explain the issue. Useful hint: don't forget to use the word 'because' in your answer! For example, in this case you could write: '*One reason why people supported abolition by 1807 was because of the successful resistance of the slaves themselves.*' [1 mark]

You can gain additional marks if you give extra information to support a point you are making. In this way you could gain 6 marks for making four relevant points and one point which you have developed with more information. For example, here you might write: '*People were influenced by complaints from fearful plantation owners about the hostility and stubbornness of their slaves.*' [1 extra mark]

Source A is from an article in BBC *History* magazine (2007) by historian James Walvin.

SOURCE A

Oddly, the abolitionist cause was given an unexpected boost by the rise of Napoleon and his efforts to restore French slavery. It was the perfect opportunity for abolitionists to assert British superiority over the French. The Foreign Slave Trade Act of 1806 had the effect of abolishing two thirds of Britain's slave trade. Traders and planters were caught completely unawares. The Lords spoke strongly against it but the old political stumbling block, William Pitt, was dead and was replaced by Lord Grenville, who was both abolitionist and able to influence events in the [House of] Lords. To cap it all, the general election of 1806 saw large numbers of abolitionist MPs returned to Westminster.

2 Evaluate the usefulness of Source A as evidence of the reasons for the abolition of the slave trade in 1807. (You may want to comment on who wrote it, when they wrote it, why they wrote it, what they say and what has been missed out.) (5 marks)

Remember, there are three ways to gain marks when you are answering this type of question. First, comment on *who* wrote it, *when* and *why* it was written. Second, comment on the information that is *in* the source. Finally, comment on anything which makes the source *less* useful, such as important information that has been left out. It is very important that you keep repeating the phrases 'this source is useful because' or 'this source is less useful because', otherwise you won't get the marks you are aiming for.

When did slavery end?

The slave trade was abolished by the British Government in 1807. In 1834, slavery was made illegal throughout the British Empire. Brazil was the final country involved in the Atlantic trade to abolish slavery, in 1888. However, slavery still exists in the world today.

Cocoa harvesting in West Africa

A young boy working on a cocoa farm owned by a neighbour in Côte d'Ivoire in 2007

Instead of going to school, some young boys are forced to spend long days cutting open cocoa pods to supply the chocolate industry. The work is very dangerous and can lead to injury and ill-health.

Cotton production in Uzbekistan

Thousands of men, women and children in Uzbekistan are forced to work harvesting cotton. Some of this cotton finds its way into European shops.

Women pick cotton near the town of Andijan, Uzbekistan, in 2005

Slavery in the UK

Slavery still exists in the UK. For example, there are estimated to be around 5000 victims of human trafficking in the UK at any one time. Traffickers arrange for people to enter the UK with the promise of a good job. Instead, the victims are forced to pay off their 'debt' to the trafficker by working long hours in unpleasant jobs. Some are forced to work in the sex industry.

This picture is posed by a model, but slavery still exists in the UK today

Additional resources

You can find out more about the existence of slavery in the twenty-first century through these websites.

‣ www.antislavery.org/english/slavery_today
‣ www.theguardian.com/uk-news/gallery/2018/jan/17/the-invisible-people-modern-slavery-in-pictures
‣ www.freetheslaves.net

'Do we get to watch *Roots* ...?'

In 1976, a retired US coastguard and former civil rights campaigner, Alex Hayley, published a book that traced his own life history back to an African called Kunte Kinte. *Roots: The Saga of an American Family* became a television mini-series and drew a massive audience of over 130 million people.

Watching *Roots* can help you to understand what life in Africa may have been like at the time of the Atlantic slave trade. However, if you watch *Roots* to help you understand this topic, you must be aware of a number of drawbacks.

> What do you think might be the dangers of using *Roots* to find out the truth about slavery?

Photographs from the television series Roots, *which was transmitted between 1977 and 1988*

The topic you are studying for the National 5 examination relates to the British slave trade, which involved the West Indies and the production of sugar. *Roots* is about tobacco and cotton plantations in Virginia, USA. Conditions on a West Indies sugar plantation were much worse than those on a Virginia plantation. So, be careful when watching *Roots*. It gives an impression of how the Atlantic slave trade operated but it does not tell the story about the West Indies, sugar or how slavery was finally ended in the islands of the Caribbean Sea.

Glossary

A

Abolitionists – people who wanted to end the slave trade

Amendment – a paragraph added to a Bill, usually by MPs

Arawak – a native people of the West Indies

Auction – a public sale at which 'lots' are sold to the highest bidder

B

Bilboes – an iron bar with sliding shackles attached that can be used to hold someone by the ankles

Bill – an idea for a law

Billhook – a long pole with a metal hook on the end

Bond servants – people forced to work for a period of time

Bonny – an area of West Africa which now includes the countries of Nigeria, Cameroon, Equatorial Guinea, São Tomé and Gabon

Branding – burning a mark into a person's skin

C

Cannibals – people who eat human flesh or organs

Cargo – the valuable contents of a trading ship

City, The – the important financial district of London

Clarkson, Thomas – a graduate from the University of Cambridge who became deeply involved in the abolitionist movement

Commodity – a product that can be bought or sold

Cugoano, Ottobah – an African abolitionist who was enslaved in Grenada but became free when he was taken to London

D

Dahomey – a country in West Africa now known as Benin

Driver – the person put in charge of a group of slaves (where the term 'slave driver' comes from)

Dropsy – a build-up of fluid within the body, leading to swelling and pain

Dysentery – an infection affecting the intestines causing severe diarrhoea

E

Entrepreneur – someone who is prepared to take risks in business

Equiano, Olaudah – an Ebo African who was enslaved in Barbados but bought his freedom and became an abolitionist

Evangelical – a strict follower of the teachings of the Bible and the importance of doing the right thing

F

Factor – an employee of a European trading firm, who gathered slaves on the coast to supply to slave ships

Financial services – services involving money like banking, credit and insurance

Flogging – whipping given as a punishment

Forts – strong stone buildings along the African coast, often used as slave factories

French Revolution – the uprising of the French people against their king

G

Gastroenteritis – severe inflammation of the stomach and intestines

Gold – a precious metal sought after by European explorers in Africa in the fifteenth and sixteenth centuries

Gradual abolition – getting rid of the slave trade slowly

Grenville, Lord – the British prime minister at the time of the abolition of the slave trade in 1807

H

Haiti – the first country in which slaves rose up against their masters and took over

I

India – a country in the British Empire that produced sugar without the use of slaves

Industrial Revolution – the rapid development of industry that took place in Britain in the late-eighteenth and nineteenth centuries

Insurers – people who pay the cost of an insurance claim

Islam – the religion of Muslims, who believe in Muhammad and worship Allah

Ivory – elephant tusk sought after by European explorers in Africa in the fifteenth and sixteenth centuries

L

Leprosy – a contagious disease affecting the nerves and skin

Lobbied – tried to persuade an elected representative

L'Ouverture, Toussaint – the leader of the freed slaves in Haiti

M

Malaria – a deadly disease passed on by mosquito bites

Manacled – confined using a metal chain to fasten the captive's wrists together

Mandingo – a tribe of people who lived in West Africa

Merchants – people who make a living from buying and selling

Middle passage – the journey from West Africa to the West Indies, the second part of the triangular trade route

Middlemen – people employed to get slaves and sell them on to Europeans

Mulatto – a term used during slavery to describe a person with one white and one black parent (now offensive)

N

New World – the area of the Americas discovered by Europeans in the fifteenth century

Newton, John – a slave ship captain who became a church minister and an abolitionist. He wrote many hymns, including 'Amazing Grace'.

O

Overseer – a person employed by a plantation owner to be in charge of slaves

P

Parliamentary inquiries – meetings of MPs with the aim of finding out more about an issue to report back to parliament

Petitions – written proposals backed by a large number of signatures

Pitt, William – the British prime minister between 1783 and 1801 and again from 1804 until his death in 1806

Plantation – an estate where crops such as coffee, tobacco or sugar are grown

Profit – money earned from making a deal where the amount received is more than the amount spent

Public opinion – the attitude of the people

Q

Quakers – a Christian group, started in the seventeenth century, that was devoted to peaceful ideas

R

Resistance – fighting back

Runaway slaves – slaves who leave the owner's property without permission

S

Salt fish – fish preserved with salt; a common food for enslaved people in the West Indies

Scarlet fever – a disease that causes fever and a scarlet rash, spread by bacteria

Scramble – a public sale where buyers rush forward to claim the 'lots' they wish to buy

Shackled – confined using a metal chain to fasten the captive's ankles together

Sharp, Granville – a man who worked for the government but became involved in trying to free enslaved people in England and became one of the first abolitionists

Ship's surgeon – the person on board a ship with some medical training (on slave ships this was often very limited)

Slave factories – places where factors carried out their business

Slave rebellions – where many enslaved people rose up against their masters

Smallpox – a serious, contagious disease caused by a virus

Sons of Africa – a group of African abolitionists that met in London during the eighteenth century

Sugar boycott – a campaign in the nineteenth century to stop people buying slave-produced sugar

Sugar cane – a tropical plant with a thick stem from which sugar can be extracted

T

Tallies – a mark or label to aid counting

Ticket – a piece of paper signed by a slave owner giving permission for a slave to do something

Trade goods – goods carried by a ship to exchange for other goods at the next destination

W

Wedgwood, Josiah – a Quaker and wealthy pottery owner who supported the abolitionist movement

West Indies – islands of the Caribbean Sea

Wilberforce, William – a Member of Parliament (MP) who made speeches and introduced Bills against the slave trade

Y

Yellow fever – a tropical disease affecting the liver and kidneys, spread by a virus

Index

Acknowledgements

p.1 extract from 'Why the progeny of slaves will strike gold at the Olympics' by John Naish in *Daily Mail* 3/07/2012; **pp.5 & 20** extracts from *The Slave Trade* by Josephine Kamm (Collins Educational, 1983); **pp.5, 20, 45 & 52** extracts from *The Slave Trade* by James Walvin. Copyright © 2011 James Walvin. Reprinted by kind permission of Thames & Hudson Ltd., London; **p.6** extract from *The Trade in White Labour in 17thC Bristol* by Andrea Button taken from http://humanities. uwe.ac.uk/bhr/Main/white_labour/conditions.htm; **pp.12, 45 & 53** extracts from *The Transatlantic Slave Trade* by David Killingray (1987). Reproduced with kind permission of B.T. Batsford, part of Pavilion Books Company Limited; **p.20** extract from 'The Story of Africa: African Slave Owners' from www.bbc.co.uk (http://tinyurl.com/qsfcge) © BBC; **p.20** extract from 'Slavery in Africa' from www.discoveringbristol.org.uk/slavery/people-involved/enslaved-people/enslaved-africans/ africa-slavery/ © Bristol City Council; **p.22** two extracts from *Satan's Kingdom* by Pip Jones (Past & Present Press, 2007). Reproduced with permission of Past & Present Press; **p.22** extract from 'The Story of Africa: The Roots of Slavery' from www.bbc.co.uk (http://tinyurl.com/6wpl3) © BBC; **pp.22, 45, 46, 49 & 52** extracts from *Slavery and the British Empire* by Morgan (2008) 117w from pp.68, 73–75. By permission of Oxford University Press; **p.22** extract from *Atlas of Slavery* by James Walvin (Routledge, 2005). Reproduced by permission of Taylor & Francis Group; **pp.32 & 35** extracts from *To the Ends of the Earth: Scotland's Global Diaspora, 1750–2010* by T.M. Devine (Penguin Books, 2011); **p.33** quote from Professor Geoff Palmer; **p.33** extract from *Scotland and the Slave Trade* by the National Trust for Scotland taken from www.nts.org.uk/learn/ downloads/Scotland%20and%20the%20SlaveTrade.pdf © 2011 the National Trust for Scotland; **p.34** extract from 'Personalities: Jean Holmes' by Irene Maver from www.theglasgowstory.com/ story/?id=TGSBH13; **p.34** extract from *It Wisnae Us: The Truth About Glasgow and Slavery* by Stephen Mullen (The Royal Incorporation of Architects in Scotland, 2009); **p.41** extract from 'Enslavement' by Mintz, S., & McNeil, S. (2018). Digital History. Retrieved August 2018 from www.digitalhistory.uh.edu/disp_textbook.cfm?smtid=2&psid=3033; **pp.45, 48, 49, 51, 52 & 53** extracts from *The Slave Trade* by Hugh Thomas. Copyright © Hugh Thomas, 1997, used by permission of The Wylie Agency (UK) Limited; **pp.47, 51 & 95** extracts from *The Slave Trade* by Tom Monaghan (Evans Brothers, 2008); **pp.47 & 54** extracts from 'The Middle Passage' taken from *Recovered Histories* www.recoveredhistories.org/storiesmiddle.php; **p.49** extract from 'The Middle Passage' taken from *The Abolition Project*, http://abolition.e2bn.org/slavery_44.html. Reproduced by permission of East of England Broadband Network; **p.95** quote from Rosemary Rees, author and History examiner; **p.95** excerpt from James Walvin (© James Walvin) is printed by permission of United Agents (www.unitedagents.co.uk) on behalf of James Walvin; **p.95** quote from David Killingray, Professor of History, University of London; **p.96** extract from *The Black Jacobins: Toussaint L'Ouverture and the San Domingo Revolution* by C.L.R. James (Penguin, 2001). Copyright © C.L.R. James, 1938, 1963, 1980; **p.96** extract from 'Robin Blackburn interview: What really ended slavery?' Taken from *International Socialism* issue 115, 2 July 2007 (http://isj.org.uk/robin-blackburn-interview-what-really-ended-slavery/); **p.97** excerpt by James Walvin from *BBC History Magazine* (© James Walvin, 2007) is printed by permission of United Agents (www.unitedagents. co.uk) on behalf of James Walvin.